THE NEXT LEAP
IN PRODUCTIVITY

WHAT **TOP MANAGERS**
REALLY NEED TO KNOW
ABOUT **INFORMATION TECHNOLOGY**

THE NEXT LEAP IN PRODUCTIVITY

ADAM KOLAWA, PH.D.

WILEY

John Wiley & Sons, Inc.

Published by John Wiley & Sons, Inc., Hoboken, New Jersey.
Published simultaneously in Canada.

For general information on our other products and services, or technical support,
please contact our Customer Care Department within the United States at
800-762-2974, outside the United States at 317-572-3993 or fax 317-572-4002.

Wiley also publishes its books in a variety of electronic formats. Some content that
appears in print may not be available in electronic books.

For more information about Wiley products, visit our Web site at http://www.
wiley.com.

Library of Congress Cataloging-in-Publication Data

Kolawa, Adam.
  The next leap in productivity : what top managers really need to know about
information technology / Adam Kolawa.
    p. cm.
  Includes bibliographical references and index.
  ISBN 978-0-470-39811-1 (cloth)
  1. Information technology—Management   I. Title.
  HD30.2.K654 2009
  004.068—dc22

                                                              2008040309

Printed in the United States of America

10 9 8 7 6 5 4 3 2 1

*This book is dedicated to the employees of
Parasoft. Thank you for all of
your hard work and good ideas.*
—Adam Kolawa

CONTENTS

FOREWORD

Don't Get Too Comfortable with the Idea that IT Is Just a Commodity

By Gary Beach

Publisher Emeritus of CIO *Magazine*

How much should top management really care about information technology (IT)? That's the question Adam bluntly poses in this feisty and compelling book. Most of the chief executive officers (CEOs) I've met, and lots of chief information officers (CIOs), too, say they really care only about business results. They've grown comfortable saying stuff like, "IT is just a utility. It's a fact of life, like air conditioning and running water."

There was a time when I would have agreed wholeheartedly. I would have joined the chorus singing, "IT is a commodity, just like electricity." But I'm less certain now. And I get uneasy when I hear people telling me over and over that nothing counts except "results."

Here's why it makes me itch when people talk about how little they care about IT and how much they care about results: You can't achieve the results you want without IT.

Sure, there are parts of IT that have been commoditized. But there are broad, sweeping swathes of IT that still represent purely creative and incredibly valuable intellectual capital that's been captured and painstakingly translated into software code.

There are plenty of companies out there competing on the basis of their IT superiority, or at the very least on the basis of their IT competency. That's a fact.

So I think the simple answer to Adam's question is this: Top management should care about IT because superior IT is a competitive advantage in a networked global economy.

The more complex answer is that top managers need to learn more about IT so they can make absolutely certain that the CIO receives the support and funding that he or she needs to run a superior IT shop.

After all, if you believe there is a connection between superior IT and superior business results, then supporting your local CIO is clearly a business imperative, right?

Adam's book is a challenge to all the top managers who've stopped caring about IT. His message is simple: If you really care about your business, you find ways to make IT more productive. The improvements you achieve in IT productivity can then be leveraged into huge leaps in productivity at the enterprise level.

This book offers a road map for translating IT productivity into business profit. Adam's argument is worth reading and worth considering as you formulate your IT strategies and plan your IT budgets.

INTRODUCTION

A Blueprint for Improving Corporate Productivity

By Michael Minelli
Coauthor of Partnering with the CIO

Adam Kolawa was trained as a theoretical physicist. His involvement in the software industry resulted from one of those strange twists of fate that happens more frequently in fiction than in real life.

About 30 years ago, Adam was struggling to calculate the mass of a glueball, a highly mysterious subatomic particle composed entirely of gluons, which are the infinitesimally tiny elementary particles that make it possible for protons and neutrons to stick together in atomic nuclei.

As you can imagine, the calculations were extremely complex and required an enormous amount of computing power.

But Adam couldn't find the right software to perform his calculations. Instead of using something that "sort of worked," but was not quite exactly what he needed, he decided to build his own software.

Adam's fateful decision pretty much ended his career as a theoretical physicist. When other people found out about his software—and about the radical approach he had invented for developing high-quality software very quickly—they beat a path to his door.

Adam eventually went on to launch Parasoft, a software company that has survived, thrived, and remained independent for more than two decades.

I must admit that I was never much interested in theoretical physics, much less gluons and glueballs. But I do know something about selling software.

In 2007, I coauthored *Partnering with the CIO* (John Wiley & Sons, 2007), a book about the challenges of selling enterprise software. The book combined journalism, research, and my personal experiences as a successful software sales executive. Let me share some of what I learned and wrote in the book with you now, because it is relevant to Adam's message.

Like all consumers, CIOs suffer buyer's remorse. Before the ink on the contract is dry, they begin worrying about whether the software they just bought will work as promised.

The key question rolling through the mind of every CIO who purchases software is: What happens after the sale?

I didn't make this up. A survey conducted recently by *CIO* magazine shows that of the 10 vendor attributes considered most important by CIOs, the ability to deliver on promises ranks number one.

Ninety-six percent of the CIOs who responded to the survey chose "vendor delivers on promises" as the most important vendor attribute. But only 54% of the CIOs agreed that vendors actually keep their promises, which is outrageous when you consider the billions of dollars spent annually on IT projects.

Clearly, there are huge gaps between the expectations of buyers and the reality of the software-purchasing experience.

The survey also hints at a far deeper problem: Many vendors do not have the capabilities or the resources to fix problems that arise in the software they sell.

Nobody expects software to be perfect. But people who purchase software expect the people who sell software to stand behind their promises.

Here is where Adam's concepts are absolutely crucial. Software vendors and CIOs who read this book will discover a software development process that is transparent, practical, and efficient. Nontechnical-level executives (CEOs, chief financial officers [CFOs], chief operating officers [COOs], etc.) will discover a blueprint for improving corporate productivity and dramatically reducing operating costs.

Part of what Adam is preaching is the importance of standards and the dangers of pursuing ad-hoc technology strategies. But another element of Adam's argument is simpler, and possibly more profound.

I think that Adam is laying the groundwork for a common language that can be used to bridge the chasms between IT and other essential components of the business, such as finance, product development, sales, marketing, distribution, and customer service.

Everyone who reads this book will learn valuable lessons that can be leveraged to improve returns on human capital investments at every level of the organization. Adam's concepts have the potential to boost levels of confidence and performance throughout the enterprise.

So if you believe that innovation is a key factor in determining success and that IT is a key enabler of innovation, this book will be an invaluable guide as you make critical business decisions about purchasing, developing, or deploying IT.

PREFACE

When I began writing this book in 2007, my goal was to generate a short text that would help CEOs and other top managers develop a better understanding of the basic concepts of information technology (IT). The limited scope of my intentions was captured succinctly in the book's original title, *Demystifying Information Technology.*

But there are unexpected twists and turns in any creative endeavor. As I wrote, I realized that my original premise was too narrow. I also realized that many of the straightforward messages that I initially had planned to present would be more valuable if I explained the foundational principles beneath them in greater detail.

Gradually, the book now before you emerged. In truth, it is really two books melded into one. The first book is about IT strategy; the second book is about IT tactics. I recommend that you read both, and I guarantee that you will learn something new from each.

As someone with a doctorate in physics, I cannot help but see the world through the prism of my academic training. So whenever I observe a discontinuous change, a virtually instantaneous increase in some value or other, I tend to call it a *quantum leap,* a term borrowed from the revolutionary

theory of quantum mechanics, which was one of the signature scientific advancements of the twentieth century. In
layman's terms, a quantum leap is any radical improvement
from an initial condition to a new and better condition, without any intermediate steps.

In this book, I am going to talk about two "quantum
leaps" that occur when IT is properly understood and properly managed.

The first such quantum leap, which I call the Developer
Leap, describes the radical improvement in the productivity of individual programmers and programmer teams when
they build software the proper way.

The second quantum leap, which I call the Enterprise
Leap, describes a radical improvement in the productivity
of the entire enterprise that can arise, with proper executive
action, after the first leap has occurred.

The point of this book, in a nutshell, is to explain what
C-level executives need to know to take advantage of this
tremendous opportunity.

ACKNOWLEDGMENTS

It would be difficult to quantify the amount of original thinking required to produce this book. Suffice it to say that many long hours were spent developing, refining, and articulating the ideas presented on the pages that follow.

I extend my thanks to Mike Barlow and John Sundman for supporting my efforts to create a manuscript that is simultaneously fresh, original, and readable. I also thank Kirsten Sandberg of Harvard Business School Press for suggesting the "quantum leap" analogy to me over breakfast at the Harvard Club while I was at the beginning stages of the writing process.

I also thank Cynthia Dunlop, our lead technical writer at Parasoft, for translating my random thoughts into clear prose. Additionally, I want to thank Wayne Ariola, Erika Delgado, Elizabeth Espinosa, Liz Garcia, Wayne Gillikin, Mark Johnson, Arthur Hicken, Marek Kucharski, Marek Pilch, and Sergei Sokolov.

This book also required many hours of research and old-fashioned journalism. I could not have written it without the knowledge and experience of many expert sources, including Gary Beach, Michael Blake, Andy Chessin, Paul Cosgrave, Rob Gingell, Paul Johnson, Mark Lutchen, Harvey

Koeppel, Marjorie Magner, Brian Margolies, Michael Minelli, and Ron Rose.

To them I am indebted deeply. I thank them sincerely for sharing their time, their energy, and their accumulated wisdom.

All writers need many additional pairs of eyes. I was fortunate to work with Edith G. Barlow, whose careful copy editing and useful suggestions greatly improved the quality of the text. Diana Zitnay's excellent transcriptions of our conversations and interviews were very helpful.

I also thank Sheck Cho and Stacey Rympa, my editors at John Wiley & Sons. Their belief in the value of my project encouraged my own personal leap as an author.

THE NEXT LEAP
IN PRODUCTIVITY

Chapter 1

Success Depends on Innovation and Innovation Depends on Information Technology

"Past results are not a guarantee of future performance. As we enter the process-centered age, this caveat should be writ large—for individuals, for companies, and for countries. It should be emblazoned on the desk of every employee, and of every citizen."

—Michael Hammer

Executive Summary

In competitive markets, innovation is the prerequisite for success. IT enables innovation. Meeting demand for innovative products and services in fast-moving global markets requires C-level executives to work more closely with IT than ever before. IT needs formal development standards and improved management practices to guarantee that new products and services will delight and amaze customers.

Another Day at the Racetrack

Rapid, unrelenting change is the price we pay for enjoying the fruits of modernity. Fresh danger and new opportunity appear suddenly, demanding immediate responses.

As recent history demonstrates, nothing can fully prepare us for the pace, complexity, and unpredictability of modern global markets. So we rely on increasingly powerful information technology (IT) to support the strategies that we invent to achieve our goals.

Without IT, we could not hope to capitalize on openings and dodge threats as they materialize. Responding quickly and effectively to changes in markets, however, requires deep portfolios of highly adaptable IT resources.

Quite frankly, IT has to be capable of changing as swiftly as the markets. A static set of IT resources will not help an organization competing in a global business environment.

But an adaptable IT system requires adaptable software. This presents both a dilemma and an opportunity.

Organizations that learn how to convert knowledge and intelligence into programming code quickly and efficiently will enjoy competitive advantages over rivals with slower, less efficient software development processes.

In the next round of global competition, having the smartest people won't be enough. What will be needed? The fastest and most creative programmers to convert your ideas into code?

Actually, no. This is an old (and dangerous) way of thinking. It assumes that IT is merely a cost incurred to support the enterprise. In fact, IT can be an incredible asset to the organization—an invaluable driver of growth and expansion. That's what this book is all about.

Winning the Race with Two Leaps in Productivity

A huge untapped potential for productivity improvement is locked up by the interoperability of IT and the other parts of the business.

But don't expect IT to unlock this potential all by itself. In fact, don't even expect IT to realize that this low-hanging fruit is there. It will continue to lie untapped until the chief executive officer (CEO) leads the charge. That is why Chapter 2 explains how to drive IT strategy from the top.

Achieving this Enterprise Leap in productivity is the responsibility of you, the CEO, the top manager of the entire enterprise. Too many people (and too many books) focus on improving the effectiveness of IT without situating that goal in the context of improving the effectiveness of the organization as a whole. Focusing on IT instead of the organization as a whole leads to opportunities squandered.

As CEO, you must change how the enterprise views and uses IT. Chapter 3 explains why. It argues that IT is one of the enterprise's most valuable assets *because it is a tool of change of that drives productivity across the enterprise.*

To reap IT's potential as an agent of change, IT itself has to become more nimble, responsive, and productive. That's why IT must improve its own productivity. Chapters 4 and 5 explain how.

Once the CEO can verify that IT productivity has truly improved, then a new partnering of CEO and chief information officer (CIO) can begin. Now, the CIO becomes a source of ideas for improving productivity across the enterprise.

This leads to the second quantum leap in productivity, which occurs at the enterprise level. As Chapter 6 explains, this second leap is achieved by gluing together current human processes with computer programs.

Meeting in the Middle

Much has been written about the need for IT to develop a deeper understanding of business. For the past decade, CIOs have been urged, coaxed, counseled, and exhorted to act more like CEOs, chief financial officers (CFOs), chief operating officers (COOs), and other C-level executives.

I'm not going to argue about the wisdom of that advice. But I'm going to suggest that it's only half the story. The other half, the piece that is usually missing from conversations about innovation, competitiveness, and the opening of new markets is this: It is time for business to learn more about IT.

Specifically, it is time for CEOs, CFOs, COOs, and other C-level executives to start acting more like CIOs.

Why now? Why should top management expend the energy required to learn more about IT, a large amorphous aggregation of multiple technologies that is constantly moving, changing shape, and evolving into who knows what?

BusinessWeek Research Services recently polled 353 C-level executives spread across multiple sectors of the economy such as financial services, health care, pharmaceuticals, transportation, retail, and manufacturing. One goal of the survey was determining which factors drive C-level decisions about IT. Nearly half of the executives surveyed were CEOs and precisely one-third were CIOs.

Here is how executives ranked their top five crucial business goals for 2008:

1. Sales and revenue growth

2. Reaching new customers

3. Improving customer service and retention

4. Increasing profit margins

5. Increasing market share

In today's economy, it is virtually impossible to achieve any of those five goals without first having the capability to develop and market brilliant new products and services that your customers will absolutely adore.

Rapid innovation and first-rate product creation require tight working relationships between the C-suite and IT. You don't have to be joined at the hip, but as one CEO recently told me: "If you're not meeting daily with your CIO, you've got a problem."

Let's face reality: IT is to business in the twenty-first century what wind was to the Royal Navy in the eighteenth century, what coal was to the Industrial Revolution, what philosophy was to the Enlightenment, and what art was to the Renaissance.

Okay, you get the point. IT is essential and indispensable. Not only is IT central to every organization, it radiates through every part of the organization. IT touches everything. IT is everywhere.

Now is the time for top managers to meet their CIOs halfway and learn to walk a mile in their shoes.

A True Story—Mostly

The following story is mostly true. I can't tell you the names of the companies involved, but you can guess. There will be no prizes for guessing right, but you will have the satisfaction of knowing that even humongous companies with legions of planners, strategists, and business analysts make mistakes that your great-grandmother would never have made.

A few years back, an extremely large global technology supplier saw an opportunity to tear off and swallow a huge chunk of the market for Internet routers. The plan was simple: They would simply overwhelm the competition by throwing vast resources into new product development, marketing, and sales.

The leading maker of routers at that time was not a small company. But it wasn't nearly as large as the global technology supplier that had fixed its hungry eye on the router market.

The company that made routers had more collective experience and deeper knowledge of the market than any potential competitor. But the company had a weakness: It had no formal company-wide standards for testing the new software that it developed for its routers and other innovative products.

For years the developers at this company had enjoyed a sense of cowboy-like freedom, largely unhampered by rules or anything else that they imagined might have restricted their creativity.

The company paid a steep price for all of this unbridled creativity. It took forever to get their pioneering products and services out the door and into the hands of their eager customers. And the overall quality of its products—especially its high-end routers—ranked among the lowest in the industry.

The company's senior vice present (SVP)—the executive responsible for software development—knew that if they were going to compete head to head with a global giant, they would need to get new products and services to market much faster than in the past. That meant they would need a world-class process for developing new software quickly and cost-effectively.

So the SVP issued an edict: Henceforth, standard tests will be applied to all software. Every night, all developers will check their newly written code into an automated system, where it will be scanned for errors. Every morning, the developers will receive reports showing the previous day's errors. Before doing any new work, the developers will fix the mistakes they made yesterday.

The beauty of this process is that it assures that each day's work begins and ends with clean code. Clean code virtually guarantees that the software will work—or at least that it will not fail or begin acting strangely because of hidden defects.

The SVP's edict saved the company. It began moving new products and new services to market so quickly and so efficiently that the global technology supplier decided to rethink its plan. Ironically, the larger company now uses the same standard testing process as the smaller company.

There is one more delicious detail. When the manager who had initially championed the testing process talks to his developers, they tell him they could not imagine writing software today without a system for testing it automatically. "Can you imagine," they say, "trying to test all this code manually?"

Talk the Talk *and* Walk the Walk

When Joseph Moses Juran, a founding father of modern quality management, died at the age of 103 in early 2008, his grandson David Juran was quoted in the *New York Times* obituary: "Everyone who's in business now adopts the philosophy of quality management."

He was right, of course. What he did not say, at least not to the *Times* reporter, is that it has become all too easy to adopt the philosophy of quality management without understanding or embracing the underlying processes that Joseph Juran spent most of his life exploring and writing about.

Good quality management usually results in higher productivity. The best historical example of this is Toyota's approach to the automotive manufacturing process. With Juran's help, Toyota devised a production system in which quality management was tightly integrated with other assembly-line processes.

As a consequence, defects were found and fixed long before the finished product left the plant. More important, the defects themselves were treated as valuable clues that might reveal ways for continuously improving the efficiency of Toyota's manufacturing processes.

Well, we all know how the story ends. Toyota is now the world's number-one automaker.

Beyond the Numbers

Juran viewed quality management as more than a system of eso-
teric numerical techniques for reducing errors in manufacturing
processes. He saw quality management as a way of making the
world a better place. He was a brilliant and decent man.

Although I was trained as a theoretical physicist, I consider
myself a student of the great philosophers of modern business—visionary thinkers such as Juran, W. Edwards Deming,
and Peter Drucker.

What their teachings share, I believe, is a sense that business is about more than business results. Business is about
life. Good businesses—that is, businesses that are well organized and well managed—improve the lives of their employees, customers, and stakeholders.

Bad businesses, however, affect life negatively. When a
business is poorly organized and mismanaged, especially if it
is a large business, many people suffer.

If parts of this book seem like angry rants against misman-
agement, it is because I believe passionately in the power and
potential of a well-run business to accomplish good things.

So What Exactly Do *I* Do?

I make a kind of highly specialized software that makes it
easier for other people to make good software. My software

is used almost exclusively by software developers, so it won't hurt my feelings if you've never heard of it.

But even if you don't know the first thing about it, my software is probably helping your home computer network run faster, your online banking transactions remain secure, and your Internet phone work without sounding like you're calling from outer space.

My software increases the productivity of software development groups—by a lot. It accomplishes this by automating every part of the software development process that can possibly be automated. If you are trying to create new software quickly, that's important.

Fred Brooks, the author of a classic book on software productivity called *The Mythical Man-Month* and highly regarded professor of computer science at the University of North Carolina, wrote an article in 1986 entitled "No Silver Bullet," in which he argued that there would never again be a giant increase in programmer productivity. Only incremental improvements were possible, he said.

As depressing as that sounds, for many years Brooks was right. But his point is no longer correct; today, it is possible to achieve astonishing improvements in productivity. And not only developer productivity, but also the productivity of the whole organization, and this is the key. I know this is true because I see it every day: radical, discontinuous improvements in quality and productivity.

I don't want to bore you with the details, so here again are the two quantum leaps condensed into two bullet points:

- **Developer Leap.** You create software from reusable "building blocks" instead of reinventing the wheel every time you need a new feature or capability. This, with automation of your software development process, leads to what I am calling "disposable software." From my perspective, disposable software is any software that is easy to produce and easy to change.

- **Enterprise Leap.** Disposable software enables you to automate all the routine business processes—processes that do not require creativity—throughout your organization. This automation creates enormous savings, and equally important, the IT infrastructure that makes it possible creates an environment that fosters constant innovation and creativity.

The computer and systems science that underlies these revolutionary changes may be complex, but the fundamental concepts are not difficult to grasp. As CEO you need to understand and embrace this new discipline, and then invite the rest of your organization to follow your lead.

Productivity Trumps Quality—and for Good Reason!

In old-fashioned software shops—of which there are hundreds of thousands in existence today—the function of the "Quality" group is testing software to find bugs.

If automobile plants worked this way, the Quality group would drive each car for 10,000 miles after it came off the assembly line to make sure nothing was broken. Sounds pretty silly, doesn't it?

The right thing to do is to make sure the right processes are in place to guarantee that each car coming off the line is perfect. The attention is to the process, not to the product.

That is the approach I take in developing software tools. While I do make software that finds bugs, the general purpose of all my tools is *preventing* bugs from ever being created in the first place!

For example, in lots of places, developers like to work with prototypes that they know are buggy, just to get a feel for the problem. That is dangerous, and my tools do not allow it. Software developers use my software to check their software for bugs before it can be put anywhere where it can do damage, even in early prototype versions.

Here is another way of saying it: People use my software to make sure that the software they create actually works— before it is loaded into a router, a network server, or a mobile phone.

My software is a critical piece of their quality management process. In many instances, my software has enabled companies to leap ahead of their competitors.

Exactly What Kind of *Ware* Are We Talking About?

Software is the soul of IT, the spirit inside the machine. But the word *software* is misleading for a variety of reasons. First, it is certainly not a "ware" in any sense that we commonly understand.

Second, the word *software* was invented as a rhetorical device for drawing a clear distinction between the program running on a computer and the computer itself, which is the hardware.

In truth, software is thought captured in lines of programming code. It is the human mind—or little pieces of it, at any rate—translated into a language that a computer can understand.

Like the human mind itself, software can be very difficult to change.

People who have never written a line of code tend to believe that software is mushy and malleable. But just the opposite is true. After software has been written, released, and loaded onto an enterprise platform or onto the hard drives of 10 million personal computers (PCs), it might as well be cast in bronze.

At the risk of treading the same path as Scott Rosenberg in his excellent book, *Dreaming in Code*, it is important for people to understand that writing good software is not an easy process—it is inherently difficult. Rosenberg wisely quotes Donald Knuth's famous observation, "Software is hard."

The sheer complexity of writing software makes it like sailing or playing the violin. You can strive for perfection, but perfection will always elude you. You will make mistakes. You will find yourself wedged into dark corners with no map to guide you back into the light. It is a really messy process.

Now multiply all that messiness by 100 or 1,000—the number of developers you might need to create a large software project or to extensively modify an existing software implementation—and you begin to understand why software development is such an expensive and inefficient endeavor.

So when the IT leaders cringe at every change request, it is not because they want to stand in the way of optimizing information technology. They are just (understandably) terrified by the prospect of change. Imagine that you are the CIO of a global bank and your CFO has already told you that next year's IT budget will be slashed to the bone. Or that you are the chief technology officer (CTO) of a national retail chain that is still working the bugs out of a recently purchased customer intelligence platform. Or that you are the COO of a transcontinental railroad that is still reeling from last year's upgrade of its business performance management solution. How eager would *you* be to take on an "IT optimization" initiative considering the associated risks?

Disposable Software

Even if you hire the world's best programmers, you're likely to run headlong into deeply rooted institutional challenges. As anyone who has ever tried can tell you, modifying any aspect of a modern software program can escalate rapidly into a task of Homeric proportions.

As suggested earlier, most of today's commercial software might as well be carved in stone.

Now imagine if you had the capability to modify code so smoothly and so easily that software would be considered disposable.

Unlike disposable diapers or disposable razors, disposable software would be environmentally friendly. It would leave no trace when you discarded it. It would be the ultimate recyclable product—and it would be endlessly renewable.

Best of all, disposable software would enable organizations to respond effectively within days or even hours to changing conditions by translating the intellectual power of their human capital investments directly into executable programs.

So what is stopping us from making the logical switch from traditional software to disposable software?

The answer lies in the hopelessly outmoded way in which we manage the creation of new software.

People outside of the software business would be amazed—and quite possibly shocked—by the premodern management techniques commonly used to develop new software. The industrial manufacturing processes of the late nineteenth century are models of efficiency compared to software development methods of the twenty-first century.

It is important to remember that the original Industrial Revolution did not proceed rapidly or in a straight line. The first factories were more like collections of independent artisans working under a single roof. All the fine details of modern industry that we take for granted today evolved over the course of several centuries.

Fitfully, and with many detours along the way, the science of manufacturing gradually emerged. And it is still evolving. Today's manufacturers are struggling to catch up with the reality of a global economy that is increasingly based on the buying and selling of intangible products created from intellectual property. Who knows what challenges manufacturers will face tomorrow!

Like the manufacturing sector, the finance sector continuously adjusts its processes to accommodate new global realities. Although you would not believe it from reading the headlines, banks and other financial institutions actually do a fairly good job of keeping pace with changing times.

Software developers cannot make the same claim. Many are still caught in a preindustrial time warp.

What the world needs now is a quantum leap in software development efficiency. If we can bring software development processes into the twenty-first century, the rest will be easy.

In the next couple of pages, I hope to show you why disposable software is not a frivolous utopian luxury, but an absolute necessity.

Only a Fool . . .

With the exception of some highly publicized foul-ups by Microsoft, most consumer software releases are nonevents. By the time a new piece of software or a new device containing a new piece of software reaches you, it is usually safe to assume that it will work pretty much as advertised.

Unless you are really unlucky, getting a new cell phone up and running does not require a lot of effort. You figure out which friends, relatives, and coworkers to put in your contact list, you choose your ring tones, you change the wallpaper, and you're good to go.

The situation is only slightly different in the commercial world, where most software applications either function properly right out of the box or require relatively simple modifications to function properly.

The picture changes at the enterprise level, where hundreds of software applications must work in constant harmony to sustain the enormous needs of a large organization or business.

Again, with the exception of a few spectacular hiccups, most enterprise software applications run smoothly and uneventfully for many years.

And that is the problem right there.

Enterprise computing applications are so complex that when they are running smoothly, only a fool would try to modify them. Even if you manage to convince the CIO that a major modification is absolutely necessary to achieve a significant business objective, the CIO's IT team will struggle furiously to resist anything but modest and mostly superficial changes in the existing system.

They will not resist change because they are hopeless Luddites—they will resist change because they know from bitter experience that even the smallest alteration in a complex IT environment will likely trigger a cascade of unexpected and hugely expensive consequences.

They also know in their bones that *any change in the system can easily make things a whole lot worse!*

No matter what the IT vendor or software consultant says, the truth is this: Every system modification requires a significant investment of money, time, and effort.

As a result, proposed software modifications that could streamline operations and enable more effective allocation of resources are often vetoed because the steep cost of change is perceived to outweigh the potential benefits.

Even if you work for a privately owned company and you do not have to worry about Wall Street analysts breathing down your neck, it is still hard to make the business case for a project with high initial costs and a long payback period.

So the leaky roof does not get fixed until there's a flood of water pouring through the ceiling.

True IT Productivity

Let's back up for a moment and examine the parameters of the challenge I have just described. Your IT team will try desperately not to let you break what is already working—even if it means sacrificing real opportunities for streamlining operations, opening new markets, growing revenue, and increasing profitability.

Faced with this degree of resistance, what are your options? You could fire your IT team and hire new employees—who would quickly become indistinguishable from the old employees.

You could outsource your IT operations—and spend the remaining years of your career worrying about business continuity, security, and a host of other pesky issues that do not vanish merely because your IT department is now spread out over five continents.

Or you could deal with the problem directly at its source: You could improve the efficiency and reliability of your software development process.

If your software development processes were brought into the twenty-first century, there is a good chance that your IT team would lose its fear of change—because they would trust the processes that create or modify software.

When complex software systems can be changed, improved, or modified easily, you have achieved what I call true IT productivity. Anything short of true IT productivity is a sham—an illusion of stability that represents the temporary calm between storms.

True IT productivity enables continuous improvement. It requires a formal, standardized, and largely automated framework for fine-tuning software development life cycles. It is an ongoing, iterative process that has no beginning and no end. It becomes standard operating procedure by force of habit.

To see the value of true IT productivity, let's look briefly at an example of what happens when IT productivity collapses.

Plunging into Crisis

As many residents of California already know, the Los Angeles Unified School District experienced a meltdown of its new $95 million payroll system. *Los Angeles Times* reporter Joel Rubin wrote this vivid description of the mess:

> … *[C]onsultants hired to implement the system urged the district to proceed as scheduled in early January 2007…they urged the district in a report to "Go! Proceed…and go-live on January 1!"*
>
> *Go live they did, plunging the district into a crisis from which it is only now emerging. Over the course of last year, taxpayers overpaid an estimated $53 million to some 36,000 teachers and others, while thousands more went underpaid or not paid at all for months.*

Marla Eby, director of communications for the teachers' union, told blogger Michael Krigsman that while the old payroll system was complex, it did work. The new system, she told Krigsman, "was rolled out too quickly, and without sufficient testing. The union requested that the system be run in parallel prior to full rollout, to ensure these problems would not occur. The school district chose not to follow this advice for budget reasons, which is ironic given all the cost overruns now."

In a better world, the school district's new payroll system would have been thoroughly tested before going live. After going live, the system would have been subjected to continuous testing. When problems surfaced, modifications would have been created, tested, and dropped into place seamlessly.

Make no mistake—problems always arise. That is the nature of complex IT systems. And, by the way, the Los

Angeles Unified School District's new payroll system was not an ad-hoc affair thrown together by amateurs. The software was supplied by SAP, the world's leading enterprise resource planning (ERP) vendor. Additionally, the district awarded Deloitte Consulting a $55 million contract to customize the software, the *Los Angeles Times* reported.

The huge costs of the new system no doubt contributed to the slow pace of fixing the problems. School officials were simply terrified by the real possibility that any modifications could easily make things even worse and wind up costing the district more money.

The result was a state of paralysis and confusion. In some instances teachers went without pay for months. Imagine being a student during that year!

We know the details of this sad story because the school district is a public entity and is subject to intense public scrutiny. As a long-time developer of enterprise software, I can testify that such situations are not limited to the public sector. The CIOs of companies in disparate industries such as travel, leisure, gaming, retail, heavy manufacturing, pharmaceutical, and health care have all shared similar stories with me.

The problem has caused considerable embarrassment, in addition to huge losses of capital, in the financial services sector. Despite spending billions of dollars to implement forward-looking financial management software systems, no single institution accurately predicted the scope and severity of dysfunction in the world's credit markets following the collapse of the real estate bubble.

Complex enterprise systems proved incapable of coping with even the most straightforward issues. For example, all major trading institutions rely on monitoring software to issue alerts when danger looms. Clearly, those systems failed—most spectacularly in the case of Société Générale, where one rogue trader lost $7.2 billion before the bank caught on.

These software failures did not occur all at once. There were signs along the way. But modifying the software would have required significant investments of operating capital. Instead, the CIOs at many leading firms were instructed to reduce their requests for capital spending and trim their operating budgets.

In hindsight, it is easy to see how such investments would have appeared trivial compared to the trillions of dollars in financial losses suffered throughout the global economy.

Managing Creativity in the Real World

Economic slowdowns offer us an opportunity to reflect and to plan for the future. Any serious planning must include a sincere drive to increase true IT productivity.

I believe that the next significant jump in worker productivity will be preceded by a leap in true IT productivity. But we will need to have a new generation of software development processes in place before the next economic "boom" gives everyone another good excuse to ignore the problem. That means we have to get busy now.

One of the thorniest issues facing software developers is human nature, or more precisely, our prejudices about the way we deal with creativity.

As a species, we tend to believe that creative processes are inherently individualistic. We are not accustomed to organizing creative processes and we often assume that creativity itself is largely unmanageable, as if it were a force of nature beyond our control.

When we think of creativity in the sciences, we imagine the lonely inventor in a cluttered workshop or the mad scientist in an isolated castle.

We do not imagine teams of individuals with different strengths and varying degrees of talent. Instead, we see a solitary genius with a global view, a Renaissance man with every possible skill required to get the job done . . . all by himself. What a guy!

I am embarrassed to admit that this delusion is especially prevalent among software developers.

What is missing from the lone-inventor fantasy is the reality of collaboration, which depends on many people with different viewpoints coming together to solve a complex problem.

No single individual on the team knows everything. Each individual understands a small part of the problem and each interacts with other members of the team. They share their knowledge, explain their insights, report their progress, and throw around ideas.

Eventually, the problem is solved as a result of continuous interaction among individual members of the team.

Superconductivity as Metaphor

Before I became a software designer, I was a theoretical physicist. So it is natural for me to draw comparisons between certain aspects of software development and physics. It occurred to me recently that the phenomenon of superconductivity provides a useful metaphor for helping us understand the challenges of managing software developers.

At normal temperatures, individual electrons within a potentially superconductive material collide with the material's atomic lattice, losing energy with each collision. But if you lower the temperature of the material sufficiently, its electrons pair up and begin mimicking each other's behavior. The paired electrons act as if they are one particle.

Pretty soon, all the electrons are moving in the same direction. Their individual behavior becomes a global effect. The collisions stop and the material's electrical resistance disappears. The result is a quantum leap in conductivity.

In our metaphor, software developers are the electrons and the software development project is the lattice structure surrounding them.

Under normal conditions, the developers bounce back and forth, ricocheting haphazardly from one problem to the next. And like the electrons, they lose energy with each collision. As a group, they are inefficient and relatively unproductive.

In an enterprise dedicated to true IT productivity, however, management organizes software developers into collaborative units and promotes a style of coherent behavior that is not terribly different from the behavior of the paired electrons in our superconductive material.

As with superconductivity, however, the devil is in the details. Promoting and sustaining the kind of coherent behavior that will result in true IT productivity requires a new type of IT management infrastructure.

Last but Certainly Not Least: Sarbanes–Oxley

The Sarbanes-Oxley Act of 2002 (SOX) requires all publicly traded companies in the United States to provide extensive financial information to regulatory agencies. Many executives think that complying with this law is an expensive nuisance that provides no real benefit to anyone. There is no doubt that it puts a great demand on the IT function.

Therefore, if for no other reason than to comply with this law and the vast changes it is enforcing in financial reporting, you should want your IT staff to be a highly productive, "peak performing" group.

Goodness knows that your job as CEO is complicated enough without having to worry about breaking the law because your IT group could not provide the right data in the right format in a timely manner.

But, as you will see by the end of this book, SOX—when you look at it as I do, from the point of view of IT and business process—is not an inconvenience. Rather, it is a blessing in disguise because it forces you to do what you need to do anyway to align your business and IT processes.

In the last chapter, I will talk about how to use SOX as a forcing function to drive the vitally important improvements in IT productivity and quality that are this book's focal points. But before we can come back to this somewhat contrarian assertion, we need to look at the whole spectrum of ways in which IT needs to change. So let's get started. . . .

Chapter 2

Who Is Driving Your IT Strategy?

"Strategic information systems are designed to increase competitive advantages or to position the company in the marketplace to increase market share or sales. . . . Approximately 50 percent of these efforts fail, and even those that are spectacularly successful often take two to three years to fully implement."

—Mark Lutchen

Executive Summary

IT is absolutely central to the success of your business, but the truth is this: You don't really understand IT. Despite all the hype and hoopla about transparency, IT remains a black box, an enigma, a mystery. Why is this a serious problem? Because if you do not understand how IT works, you cannot create the proper business requirements to drive IT strategy. And if you are not driving IT strategy, then who is?

From Black Box to Runaway Train

When you consider how long information technology (IT) has been around, it is astonishing to think that most corporate executives did not learn how to operate a computer until the mid-1990s. Despite the proliferation of desktop personal computers (PCs) in the late 1980s and early 1990s, many executives perceived the bulky beige boxes as unattractive nuisances. Maybe they were okay in cubicles, but did they really belong in corner offices?

Small wonder that IT departments (or information services departments, as they were called back then) were usually relegated to basements or other out-of-the-way areas. IS staffers were generally held in low esteem. IS managers were only a notch higher on the status ladder. From the standpoint of top management, *everyone* in IS was a geek.

Information technology itself was regarded as weird and mysterious, a necessary evil. IT was a cipher, a dark art, a black box. Every year, the corporation poured a small amount of money into the black box, and every year, the corporation extracted a few small and unglamorous results, such as faster consolidation of financial data or fewer duplicate names on mailing lists.

37

Occasionally, a successful IT project would result in the automation of some routine processes, which in turn would lead to reduced headcount and lower operating costs. The triumphs of IT were usually subtle and definitely not headline news.

All that changed during the Internet bubble. All of a sudden, the geeks in IT became cool. IT was the high tide that lifted everyone's boat—especially if the boats were owned by techno-savvy venture capitalists in Silicon Valley and their lucky investors.

The fact that the bubble had not produced nearly as much wealth as everyone imagined it had, or that much of the wealth it produced vanished when the bubble burst, did not dim the glow of IT. People seemed to understand that even if the bubble was largely the result of a large-scale fantasy, the technology underneath it was real.

The emergence of powerful new programming languages accelerated the evolution of IT and democratized software development processes. Faster than anyone had anticipated, important IT capabilities jumped from corporate infrastructures and took up residence on the Web.

In a flash, it seemed, IT became ubiquitous. IT did not just live on mainframes or servers or networks. IT lived on laptops, wireless phones, personal digital assistants (PDAs), TVs, music players, toys, countless household appliances, automobiles, airplanes—IT was everywhere!

The global footprint of IT became huge, expanding beyond the comprehension or mastery of any single person or organization. As IT grew in size and complexity, an odd thing happened: The perception of IT as a dark art returned. It seemed as if IT had somehow managed to crawl back into its mysterious black box.

Once more, executives at companies large and small were left in the dust, wondering what was going on and trying to figure out how to make money—or at least avoid losing money—in this newest chapter of the continuing IT saga.

Managing IT versus Understanding IT

The reversion of IT to its old status as a dark art presents a serious problem. Few people nowadays question the critical importance of IT or doubt its role as an engine of business growth and long-term profitability. But here's the catch: Most executives say they understand IT. In truth, however, very few executives really understand how IT works.

Okay, we can all live with that. What we cannot all live with is this: Very few executives really understand how IT should be managed. That is why I wrote this book. I want to launch a serious conversation about how IT should be managed in a world in which IT plays a central role.

From our point of view, IT has become a runaway train. It is not too late to avert a wreck, but the executives and managers making the decisions are going to have to start issuing better instructions to the geeks driving the train.

Why IT Matters

Despite popular notions to the contrary, companies still spend far more on salaries and employee benefits than they spend on IT. Most corporate IT budgets are mere fractions of what is spent to run traditional functions such as sales, marketing, research and development (R&D), production, customer service, distribution, and maintenance.

That being said, the costs of IT are not trivial. Every year, more tasks are turned over to the IT department or outsourced. To an increasing extent, IT manages the outsourcing. You do not need a degree in economics to foretell that IT budgets are likely to grow as the budgets of departments shrink.

Some futurists predicted that automation and outsourcing would increase efficiency and productivity to a point at which IT spending could be safely reduced to bare minimums. In retrospect, that seems a bit like saying that when the farmer finishes plowing his fields, he can go ahead and shoot his oxen.

In any event, arguments over the costs of IT miss the point. If the first job of IT is driving down operational costs through the automation of routine tasks, its second job is helping the company achieve competitive advantages in the market through speed, agility, and consistency.

Saving money is nice, but making money is even better. When managed properly, IT helps companies make money.

Managing IT poorly, however, does more than just squander the original purchase price of the technology. Years of potential growth and profitability are sacrificed when IT investments are managed improperly or incompetently. In addition to losing vast sums of capital, companies risk losing market position, prestige, and brand equity.

For companies that depend on e-commerce, IT is fundamental to the attainment of basic business objectives. For companies whose earnings are based on constant technological innovation or time-to-market advantages, IT is an irreplaceable engine for generating revenue and profit.

That is why IT matters and why executives must either learn how to manage IT properly or face the consequences.

The Right Questions

CIOs are expected to understand the markets in which their parent corporations compete. They are expected to understand how the various business units within the corporation function and how each unit contributes to the corporation's success.

CEOs and CFOs, however, are not expected to understand how IT works. But they are expected to ask the right questions.

For example, when the CIO proposes a new IT project, top management should always ask:

1. How much money will it save the company?

2. How much will it increase operational capacity?

3. When will it be done?

After the project has been approved and is in development, top management should be asking:

1. How are we tracking against the milestones we established?

2. Are we going to miss a milestone? Why?

You don't ask these types of direct, nontechnical questions for the purpose of launching a wide-ranging conversation about all the cool stuff that IT can accomplish. You ask these questions to focus the CIO's attention on what is important: business results.

Don't wait for the CIO to drop by your office with a PowerPoint deck. Feel free to visit the IT department and look around. While you are there, ask the CIO:

1. What else are you doing to save the company money?

2. What other processes can we automate?

3. Which legacy systems can we safely kill?

The CIO should not be the only one sitting on the hot seat. There are plenty of questions that you should be asking yourself, such as:

1. What can our company realistically expect from IT?

2. How will IT performance affect other parts of the enterprise?

3. Is IT budgeting driven by business needs or something else?

If you have the time to take your CIO to lunch, here are two questions you should ask before dessert arrives:

1. Does our company have an information strategy in place?

2. Does our IT architecture support our information strategy?

Prioritizing IT

Maybe the subtitle of this book should have been "What Top Managers Really Need to Know About *Prioritizing* Information Technology," because separating what needs to be done today from what can wait until tomorrow is a huge part of managing IT.

The process of prioritizing IT will depend to a large extent on how the company views the role of IT. Many companies rely on IT to enable and improve their existing business processes.

A growing number of companies, however, regard IT as a critical weapon in a never-ending struggle for market position. So the first question that top management needs to ask itself is this: Is IT *enabling* our business, or is IT *driving* our business?

A truly responsible set of top managers might go a step beyond and ask: Do we really understand the potential of IT within our environment? Where are we on the spectrum of IT users? Are we using IT to keep the trains running, or are we using IT to create new products and open new markets?

When the role of IT is enabling or streamlining processes, top management will be asking variations of three questions:

1. Is IT operating as planned?

2. Is IT saving the company money?

3. Is IT keeping us compliant?

When IT is driving the business or when IT *is* the business, as in the case of many financial companies, top management will be asking very different questions, such as:

1. Do we have the latest and greatest technology?

2. Are we constantly optimizing all of our IT resources?

3. Do we have the right mix of technology, process, and human capital in place to achieve maximum return on investment (ROI) from our IT portfolio?

As more organizations adopt knowledge-driven or information-based growth strategies, top managers are routinely asking CIOs to answer a single blunt question: What is IT doing to grow the business?

When IT *Is* the Business

First Data Corporation, a leading provider of electronic commerce and payment solutions for businesses worldwide, is essentially a huge IT department dedicated to finance.

Think about it: First Data's portfolio of services and solutions includes merchant transaction processing services; credit, debit, private-label, gift, payroll, and other prepaid card offerings; fraud protection and authentication solutions; and electronic check acceptance services through TeleCheck, as well as Internet commerce and mobile payment solutions. The company's STAR Network offers personal identification number (PIN)-secured debit acceptance at two million ATM and retail locations.

First Data depends on IT for its existence. First Data cannot afford to take IT lightly, and it does not.

"If IT is enabling your business, then it's okay to hire the kids who got B's and C's to work in your IT department," says Michael Blake, First Data's former senior vice president for

IT finance. "But if you're in the financial services business today, you need to hire the kids who got A's, because IT is your product and you want your product to be better than everyone else's product."

Never a Dull Moment

Ron Rose, the longtime chief information officer (CIO) of Priceline.com, estimates that at any given moment in time the company is evaluating, specifying, scheduling, planning, and executing several hundred IT projects.

To cope with that workload, Priceline.com has developed its own project management disciplines for planning product and system enhancements related to specific business goals several quarters in advance.

From Rose's perspective, a primary function of top management is helping IT prioritize its portfolio of assignments. "The CEO is responsible for driving strategy," says Rose. "I'm responsible for providing the CEO with timely and cost effective alternatives."

Specifically, says Rose, IT is responsible for providing general management with accurate, comprehensive project road maps that efficiently utilize the available resources, and for creating workable processes for achieving the tactical goals within the strategy.

"What we're really talking about is a portfolio management exercise," says Rose. "In my experience, the overwhelming majority of problems encountered by knowledge-driven organizations begins with IT portfolio management and resource allocation issues."

When targets are well defined and IT resources are allocated appropriately, the business advances. When targets are poorly defined and IT resources are not made available, the business suffers.

Participate in Writing the Business Requirements

If you ask an experienced software consultant to name a basic ingredient that is common to all successful IT projects, the answer you are likely to hear is this: the right set of business requirements.

Since all IT projects begin by creating a list of business requirements, it is essential for top management to be involved in the process of generating this list. Like the questions listed earlier, business requirements are not written in technical language. Here's a list of typical business requirements:

1. Reduce production costs by 4% in 12 months.

2. Increase e-commerce transactions by 10% in six months.

3. Reduce average transaction time by 40% in nine months.

4. Increase revenue from online catalogue sales by 15% in six months.

Writing and validating business requirements is an incredibly important piece of the IT puzzle. But do not take our word for it. Kaiser Permanente, the health maintenance organization (HMO) giant based in Oakland, California, recently installed software to improve its processes for generating business requirements of new IT projects. Kaiser, which spends about $1 billion annually on IT, estimated that it would save $60 million by improving the way it defined business requirements for new systems.

Now that is a significant cost reduction. Before you start thinking, "Gee, that's a no-brainer, I'm sure we're already doing something like that at our company," please be aware that most IT organizations rely on outside consultants or business analysts to write business requirements for new IT projects. And all too often, the business requirements are written to match the capabilities of an existing solution.

That is wonderful if all you care about is how elegantly the solution works. If your goal is achieving a tangible business result, however, then you had better be involved in writing the business requirements.

In the words of Karl E. Wiegers, an IT consultant and author of several books on software requirements, "If you don't get the requirements right, it doesn't matter how well you execute the rest of the project."

Wiegers calls that a "cosmic rule." I agree, and I will take it a step further. If you are not writing the business requirements, then you are not driving IT strategy. And if you are not driving IT strategy, then who is?

It Is Your Turn to Drive

The French statesman Georges Clemenceau is often credited with observing that "war is too important to leave to the military." Would it be outrageous to suggest that IT strategy is too important to leave to the IT department?

At the risk of sounding cruel and mean-spirited, leaving IT strategy in the hands of the IT department is a little bit like letting construction workers design your house. They might do a great job. They are probably more talented than your architect. They can definitely hammer nails and saw planks of wood better than your architect. So why not hire the construction workers and save yourself a bunch of money?

Because you know it would be a bad idea. How are you and the construction workers going to communicate? What experiences do you have in common that you can use to develop a working relationship? And, by the way, the town building department is going to require an architect's signature on your plans.

How about this for a solution: if you know what you want your house to look like, design it yourself and have your architect check the plans to make sure you have not done anything really stupid or dangerous. By all means, hire the construction workers to build it.

The analogy is far from perfect, but you get the drift. If you are a chief executive or a member of senior management, you already know what you want IT to accomplish. The job of the IT department is executing on the plans that emerge from your vision.

You want results—and you do not really care about the details. As far as you are concerned, it does not matter whether IT is a black box or a lemon meringue pie—as long as IT delivers the outcome you promised your board of directors, it is okay.

What I am saying is this: If you are a top executive and you really want IT to deliver the business results that you are seeking, you need to start managing it yourself. You do not have to manage it directly or even closely—nobody likes to be micromanaged—but you cannot sit back in the first-class compartment while someone else drives the train. Those days are over.

Leadership from Above

Paul Cosgrave is commissioner of New York City's Department of Information Technology and Telecommunications. As the CIO of New York City, he oversees the city's sprawling IT infrastructure.

To date, the department's greatest feat has been completing the city's 311 system, a nonemergency "help desk" for anyone with problems or questions about city services. "We've handled 50 million calls in over four years," says Cosgrave. "It's been a huge, huge success."

The success of the 311 project is all the more remarkable because it required the city to unify the operations of approximately 40 separate agency call centers that traditionally had been handling complaints and fielding questions.

Cosgrave is quick to point out, however, that leadership for the project came from above—specifically, from New York City Mayor Michael Bloomberg.

"Organizational change requires a vision of what can and what should be done to improve business performance," says Cosgrave. "IT leaders can help business leaders express the vision. IT can be an enabler of change. But change should not be led by IT. For transformational change to really occur, the business leaders—in this case, the mayor—must express and support the vision."

Mayor Bloomberg deserves the accolades he received for the 311 system "because he personally took a leadership role in promoting and developing the system," says Cosgrave. "You need a strong leader to make real change happen."

Communicate, Communicate, Communicate . . .

After you have decided to move ahead with an IT project, fostering and supporting teamwork become absolutely crucial. Since an essential ingredient of teamwork is communication, top management needs to make certain that all stakeholders communicate constantly throughout the development process.

"At best, IT projects are filled with uncertainty," says Paul Johnson, president of Kelley Blue Book, the respected provider of automotive information. "So we try to manage the scope—and the variability of the scope—in our up-front planning, instead of trying to manage it from the development side."

But when market conditions change—and they *always* will—the project will likely change to reflect those new conditions. That is when a closely knit team proves invaluable. "Whenever possible, we try to have all the stakeholders working in the same area so that decisions can be made quickly and there's no delay in pulling together meetings," says Johnson. "You want the business owners to be available so they can answer questions in minutes or hours instead of days or weeks."

In addition to publishing its famous *Blue Book* of automotive prices, Kelley operates the leading web site for consumers searching for information they can use to get the best possible deals on automotive purchases. "Our web site attracts 13 million unique visitors per month and we deliver 250 million ads per month," says Johnson. "All of that is driven by IT."

When Kelley decided to create a new online research tool for its web site, the project team ran into constraints created by the original set of business rules written for the company's automotive database. The old rules would not allow site visitors to search the database in a way that nontechnical users would find comfortable.

Clearly, this was a critical issue for the business owner, who viewed the project from the perspective of a consumer. At another company, the business owner might have been required to explain the problem to the developers through a cumbersome and time-consuming process.

At Kelley, the issue was resolved in mere hours because the stakeholders are accustomed to communicating rapidly—and because they understand that top management values their abilities to solve problems quickly.

Chapter 3

Read My Lips:
IT Is an Asset

"An asset is a resource controlled by the enterprise as a result of past events and from which future economic benefits are expected to flow to the enterprise."

Executive Summary

Companies that treat IT as an asset will have inherent advantages over companies that treat IT as merely a cost. This is not just a question of semantics; it is an issue of fundamental beliefs and values. If you believe that IT is your company's intellectual property captured in code, then you will treat IT as an asset. If you believe that IT is a system of advanced utilities for consolidating spreadsheets and delivering email, you will find it increasingly difficult to compete in today's market.

If You Are Not an Asset, You Are a Liability

In too many businesses, information technology (IT) is still regarded as a cost, like the gas or electric bill.

This view of IT is dead wrong. It leads to faulty assumptions and poorly set priorities. It reflects a profound and potentially fatal misunderstanding of the nature of business in the twenty-first century.

So let's just state the honest truth: Companies that view IT as a cost, rather than as a fundamental embodiment of the business itself, are doomed to failure.

Even if your company has the smartest chief information officer (CIO) and the best IT department in the world, its efforts will be fruitless if it treats IT as a cost and not an asset.

An asset, by common definition, is a benefit—assets are expected to generate future net cash flows. Assets are the source of future economic gain. If you are running a business, you do not treat your assets lightly—you take care of them, you coddle them, you protect them, and you value them. They are your future.

Sadly, many conversations between the CEO and the CIO go like this:

CEO: We've got to cut costs another 3% to meet our quarterly earnings projections or the analysts will hammer us. Which IT projects can you kill or put on hold?

CIO: I'll get you a list this afternoon.

Now imagine the CEO is the defendant in a trial and he is talking to his lawyer:

CEO: Gee, this is getting more expensive than I thought it would. Do we really need all these expert witnesses?

Lawyer: Only if you want to be acquitted.

I suppose that if the lawyer had an MBA (master of business administration) in addition to his JD (doctor of jurisprudence), he might advise his client to think of the expert witnesses as assets rather than costs. He might advise the CEO to think of acquittal as a future benefit of his investment in the witnesses.

My advice to every CEO is this: Treat your CIO like gold, because your future success will depend largely on his or her performance. Treat your CIO and the IT department as strategic assets. That does not mean that you give them a free ride—in fact, it means that you need to manage them more carefully and more closely *because now you recognize just how valuable and important they really are to you.*

It's Déjà Vu All Over Again

"When I hear the words *IT department,* it brings me right back to 1970," says Mark Lutchen, former global CIO of PricewaterhouseCoopers (PwC) and currently senior practice partner for PwC's IT Effectiveness Initiative. He is also the author of *Managing IT as a Business,* one of the most useful books on IT management written in the past ten years.

Any organization that still refers to its information technology portfolio as the "IT department" is already in trouble, according to Lutchen. A "department" suggests a separate function, something that lives somewhere else.

"IT is so completely integrated into the business that it's inescapable. You cannot shut it off. You cannot move away from it. You cannot operate without it," he says.

Ideally, the CIO should function as the CEO's technology agent. The CIO is a representative of the CEO's vision, a proxy acting on the CEO's behalf.

"But the concept of the CIO serving as the CEO's proxy only works when the CEO accepts the CIO as an equal," says Lutchen. "How can I give you my proxy if I don't believe that you're just as capable as I am of making the right decisions?"

Lutchen makes an excellent point. Now I will take it a step further. A crucial part of the CEO's job is finding a CIO that he or she trusts to act as a proxy.

Allow me state this more clearly: If you do not trust your CIO to serve as your proxy, you should fire your CIO and find one you can trust to be your eyes, your ears, and your brain. You owe that much to your company.

A New Partnership

Marjorie Magner describes the ideal relationship between the CEO and the CIO as a partnership.

Magner knows a lot about the value that well-managed information technologies can bring to a large organization. Before launching a private equity firm in 2007, she was the CEO of Citigroup's Global Consumer Banking Group.

In that role, she led Citigroup's efforts to serve customers through retail banking, credit cards, and consumer finance in over 50 countries. Nearly 200,000 employees worked in her organization, which grew at a compound annual rate of 22% from 2001 to 2005.

IT was a major part of her strategy. "But it was never technology just for technology's sake. It was technology in service to the business," she explains.

The relationship between the CEO and the CIO is just as important as the relationship between the CEO and any other C-level executive, says Magner.

"I call it a partnership because you both understand what you're trying to accomplish and you're both thinking about it the same way. That doesn't mean you never disagree, but once you're out there and doing it, you're both on the same page, you're trying to make the same things happen for the business. You're doing it together."

The CEO's relationship with the CIO is especially crucial because of the many potential benefits that technology provides to the business. "Whether you're talking about delivering a product to the customer, managing your cost structure or analyzing data, IT is absolutely fundamental to the business," says Magner.

Magner attributes part of the Global Consumer Banking Group's success to the good working relationship she developed with the unit's CIO, Harvey Koeppel. "He brought me ideas and creativity, as well as an infrastructure we could depend on to achieve our goals."

Magner and Koeppel met frequently to discuss the role of IT within the business. "We were always asking ourselves, 'What is it that we're trying to do? How do we see the business? What's the future of the business? What are other people doing? How can we get from where we are today to where we want to be tomorrow?'"

Constant communication was a hallmark of the working relationship between the CEO's office and IT. "We spoke together in formal meetings and informal meetings," Magner recalls. "If it's a real partnership, you're going to chat regularly. If the only time you talk is when somebody puts it on a calendar, that's probably not a good sign."

Magner had learned FORTRAN at the beginning of her finance career. She had spent enough time writing code to be comfortable speaking directly with developers about new technology solutions.

"I would ask them, 'Are we presenting data to the customer in an understandable way? Or are we just throwing a bunch of stuff on a screen and expecting the customer to figure it out?' I'd tell them, 'The customer is not going to figure it out unless we make it easy, logical and intuitive.' I would also remind them that the system had to be easy for internal users. If our own people couldn't remember how to use the system without putting sticky notes all over their terminals, how could we expect anyone else to figure it out?"

Magner recalls that it took time and effort to explain her strategy to the developers.

"These developers were brilliant, brilliant young people and they would look at me like I had ten heads," she says with a smile. "But eventually we delivered a valuable service that customers and internal users could navigate easily and intuitively. So I always believed that the time I spent talking with the developers was worth it."

Magner says she comes from a "long line of CEOs who talk with developers. When we were developing a system at our consumer finance business, the CEO would come out to where we were developing it and he'd sit down to see what we were doing."

That CEO had two good reasons to sit with the developers, she says. "First, he was actually very interested in the process, and second, he wanted to make sure that what we were developing made sense for the business."

"When you're the CEO of a huge company, you don't always have the time to sit down with the developers, but I would argue that if what's being developed is really important for the business, you ought to spend a couple of hours with the developers. To me, that's a good use of the CEO's time."

Great Expectations

Now that we have raised the level of what IT should expect from the CEO, it is fair to ask: What should the CEO expect from his or her IT department?

"I think what a CEO should expect from IT is not to be let down, not to be disappointed and not to be surprised by failures such as poor execution or inconsistent quality," says Magner. "It's just a terrible thing to be in that breakdown mode, when nothing happens the way it should, when services aren't available to the customer or when there are errors. You've got to have 'industrial strength' IT and it's got to be dependable."

Any manager or executive who has ever been forced to deal with a network crash or a buggy Web application can agree with that easily enough. But please read her next comment carefully:

"The other fundamental issue is that IT should be imbedded into the thought process of the business. IT is part and parcel of everything you do. IT must be integrated into the way you think about the delivery of your business, the infrastructure of your business and how you're going to accomplish the goals of your business."

Magner also believes that IT should play a role in helping the CEO prepare for whatever is happening next. "IT should be a place where ideas come from, where opportunities are identified, where new stuff and novel concepts are discussed. IT should be thinking about the future."

When IT Is a Business Channel

Brian Margolies, vice president of IT planning at Scholastic Inc., remembers when IT executives were seen as caretakers of machines. "Now we're seen as innovators that companies need to survive and grow," says Margolies. "The business looks to IT for increased efficiencies that help the bottom line and innovations that grow the top line."

As one of the company's "technology strategists," Margolies needs to understand where the business will be two to three years from now. "That gives me a target to build to. I'm trying to drive change that's probably 18 to 36 months down the road."

Until very recently, publishers all followed the same business model. Acquire manuscripts and deliver them to customers in the form of printed books.

Now publishers are gearing up for momentous change. In addition to delivering content on the printed page, they will probably begin to offer a significant portion of their libraries in a variety of digital formats.

In the past, brick-and-mortar bookstores had been the company's primary sales channel. But as everyone who has ever bought a book from Amazon.com already knows, the bookstore has moved from the mall to the Web.

A shift in business strategy means that IT has to shift, too. And it also means that IT will jump from playing a supporting role in the company's revenue model to playing a starring role.

It is entirely likely that within a couple of years, IT will become a primary channel for publishing and distributing content. And if today's economic trend continues, IT might wind up as the *only* distribution channel for most content.

"IT has evolved from being purely operational to being a business partner, which makes sense because to a greater extent than ever before, IT is becoming the business," says Margolies.

Margolies also spoke about digital asset management solutions that might become the core of a new business model. "If content is delivered digitally, two things are going to happen. First, you're going to take tremendous costs out of the business. Printing, shipping, storing and then reshipping those books to customers all require tremendous amounts of money," he explains.

"Think about what you're saving if you're going to just take the digital file and deliver it directly to the customer! Those savings will go right to the bottom line. And you'll also see top-line growth because now you'll be marketing and selling digital content directly to customers who want to read books on one of the new kinds of handheld digital readers."

In this kind of business model, a book becomes more than a book—it becomes metabook that can be deconstructed and sold in chunks.

"Let's say instead of buying the whole book, you could just buy the pages your child needs to review that day's lesson or to do that night's homework. You might never buy the entire book—you might only buy the pages you need."

When your bookstore lives on the Internet, IT can track all the content that gets sold, right down to the page level. The opportunities for creating customized products and services on the fly are virtually unlimited.

The only problem is that as the business model becomes more complex and more dynamic, the burden on IT increases. Increasingly complex business models that depend on multiple business partners to deliver goods and services across multiple channels will only add to the burden.

In Chapter 5, I will look at how service-oriented architecture is helping smart IT shops manage their new responsibilities and fulfill their potential as agents of change and business transformation. But in the next chapter, I am going to shift gears and talk about issues at the developer level. Solving these issues will be critical as you move forward with any business programs that are enabled by IT.

Chapter 4

Achieving a Quantum Leap in Developer Productivity

"An ounce of prevention is worth a pound of cure."

—Ben Franklin

Executive Summary

For more than 50 years, the software industry has largely ignored the lessons of Total Quality Management. The result is dysfunctional organizational structures and lots of time and money wasted fixing problems that should never have been allowed to happen. It is time for IT organizations to catch up to their peers in manufacturing. By adopting the process-oriented techniques of automated defect prevention (ADP), any IT group can vastly improve its effectiveness. But this requires clear vision and firm leadership from the CEO because successful implementation of ADP requires cultural changes that will be resisted.

Essential Software Concepts for Top Managers

When your enterprise software is built around the right architecture, small leaps in software development productivity can lead to huge leaps in enterprise productivity. So we have two kinds of leaps:

Developer Leap—occurs at the tactical level

Enterprise Leap—occurs at the strategic level

I firmly believe that these two leaps are truly revolutionary. But in order to achieve these leaps, the internal structure of your information technology (IT) group must change. Indeed, the entire relationship of IT to the enterprise must change as well.

As CEO, you can no longer delegate all IT issues to the chief information officer (CIO). You need to know enough about software productivity that you can determine for yourself whether your IT organization, and your CIO, are up to par. You do not have to get down into the bits and bytes, but you do have to understand the key concepts.

In this chapter, we are going to look at the Developer Leap, and I will explain how to organize your IT operation to produce large amounts of high-quality software, improving productivity by as much as a factor of ten. In later chapters, we will explore the Enterprise Leap.

Quest for "Disposable Software"

In order to compete in today's marketplace, your IT group needs to be able to produce software that is relatively easy to use, works immediately, and is cheap to build. If you extrapolate each of these characteristics to its logical extreme, you arrive at the notion of software that is essentially disposable—for example, in the way that drawings made on a whiteboard are disposable.

I am not saying we are there, of course. Even in the best-run enterprises, software development is difficult. But you should always keep in your head the idealized notion of disposable software.

Until you get there, your IT infrastructure will have the feel of a sunk cost that is holding you back instead of being the liberating tool that it should be.

To Improve Quality, Focus on Productivity

I cannot emphasize enough how important it is that your IT group produce high-quality software. Every bug in software used by your business is both a problem and a symptom of a larger problem.

Defective software can cause anything from mild irritation on the part of a few users to catastrophic system failures.

In the new, open world, any number of outside entities may rely on *your* software to achieve *their* goals. I am talking about your customers, suppliers, partners, investors, and the government for starters.

Your software is going to interact with theirs. If the software that comes out of your IT group is of poor quality, you will be gumming up *their* works as well as your own. The quality standards by which you will be measured are going up, and they will continue to go up indefinitely.

But here is a paradox. If you want to improve quality, you need to focus on productivity, not quality. If you focus on quality, you will kill productivity and lose both. You need, instead, to focus on getting more work out of your development team.

If the team is more productive, its members will produce higher quality output. They will spend less time fixing bugs, which is expensive, and more time doing original design work, which is where innovation comes from. This is counterintuitive. Let me explain.

Do Not Change a Flat Tire with an Arc Welder

If you hang out with developers, you will sometimes hear them talking about a "quick-and-dirty" solution to a problem. Often, this is done by "hardwiring" or "hardcoding," which means to solve a *particular instance of problem* instead of solving the *general class of problem*.

Software engineers even have a word to describe an inelegant or pieced-together solution to an engineering task. They call it a kludge (or *kloodge*). A *kludge* is something that is ad hoc and ugly, but will do in a pinch.

Imagine that you are changing a flat tire on a construction site and lose the lug nuts when somebody accidentally knocks them down an open drain. You are stuck, with no way to hold the wheel to the car.

What to do? You might simply get somebody to weld the wheel to the axle, fusing the spare to the car. Two minutes with an arc welder, and presto, you're back in business! That would be a kludge, and I am sure you can see why it is a horrible solution to the problem.

But you can probably understand why software engineers do the software equivalent of that kind of thing. They do whatever it takes to get their "car" back on the road. The next time that car gets a flat tire, it will be somebody else's problem.

And that is exactly why the "legacy" code base in any large program is such a nightmare to maintain. It is littered with the software equivalents of wheels welded onto axles.

This ad-hoc way of producing software is no longer acceptable. You need to develop software that is reliable, flexible, understandable, and maintainable. Kludges are no longer allowed.

What Is Productivity?

This is a book about improving IT *productivity*, but I have not yet told you what I mean by the word. Okay, now I will. (Remember, here I am talking about *developer* productivity. Later, I will explain how to use the improvement in developer productivity to achieve a quantum leap in the productivity of the enterprise as a whole.)

Over time, there have been many attempts to define metrics that effectively measure software development productivity. Most of the ones that I have seen are amazingly complicated and very difficult to apply.

There is a simpler productivity metric that should be used across the industry: the total number of lines of code (LOC) in the organization divided by the number of people who work on that code. For short, I will call this metric the *LOC per head* (where "head" means "person" in business jargon).

It Is All in Your Heads

LOC per head is an excellent representation of the development organization's true productivity. If the LOC per head is high, it means that you have a relatively low number of people working on code—you are accomplishing a lot with minimal resources.

If you add more people to the project because the requirements are not being implemented fast enough, then the productivity goes down (the average LOC per head drops). That
is because the average number of LOC stays about the same
(some new code written, some stale code deleted), while
the number of developers goes up. It does not matter how
fast individual developers produce code. That is a different
issue.

It also does not matter if you are customizing a packaged
application or building an application from the ground up. You
count every line of code your team actually writes or modifies—
but not the lines of code in the actual packaged application. If
it is a line of C++ language code for a custom application
being developed in-house, you count it. If it is a line within
a script or configuration file needed to customize a packaged
application, you count it. And if it is a line of new Java code
written to integrate your packaged applications into the rest of
your IT infrastructure, you count that, too. In fact, if you look
at the LOC-per-head metric separately for each code type,
I guarantee you will find that the code written to customize
and integrate packaged applications is in fact the bane of your
IT productivity. But again, that is a different issue.

Approximately 10 to 20 thousand lines of code per developer is the norm for most of today's development organizations. This is based on the current industry averages, which
state that a typical program has about half a million lines of
code, and there are usually about 30 to 60 developers working on that code base. I can help you do much, much better
than that.

You Cannot Improve What You Do Not Understand

Development productivity depends on how fast the person can create new algorithms and represent them in the code (and eliminate poor or unneeded code). How fast the person can do this is a function of how well he or she understands correlations inside the code.

That is a crucial element of productivity: understanding the code.

Understanding of the code influences the number of lines of code a person can work with reasonably. That is why the LOC per head is so critical. The higher this number is, the more code each person understands, and the faster the application can evolve.

LOC per head is a single number: easily calculated, easily understood. And from what I have seen, this number never lies. It is an effective measure regardless of whether the LOC includes comments, and it applies equally well whether code is in maintenance or development phase. It is not perfect, but it is a reliable measure of productivity.

So, how do you increase the LOC per head?

Crucial Methodology

In order to get more work out of your IT team, you will have to incorporate them into a programming system that works like a well-oiled machine. You must create an infrastructure that includes regular procedures and lots of automation.

When you have this infrastructure set up correctly, developers are not wasting time in meetings, reviewing status, or working out schedules; they are not thrashing over interfaces being redesigned for the *n*th time; and they are not struggling to incorporate new features that were not in the original requirements.

Most importantly, when you do things the right way, developers do not have to stop what they are doing and go back to fix bugs found by quality assurance (QA) after the code has been "completed." Instead, they are doing what you are paying them to do, which is to create innovative solutions to complex business problems.

When the environment is set up correctly, it becomes almost impossible to create poor code. When software is done right, QA does not find defects for developers to fix. Rather, the defects never happen in the first place. The result: Both productivity *and* quality go up.

The way to achieve this is through a methodology that I call Automated Defect Prevention (ADP). In a nutshell, ADP is a practical approach to software management through process improvement. (For a more in-depth, technical discussion of this methodology, please refer to *Automated Defect Prevention* by Dorota Huizinga and Adam Kolawa.)

There is nothing about this approach that is rocket science. It is merely the application of proven methods of continuous process improvement to the domain of software development. These quality-improvement techniques have been used in manufacturing for more than half a century, but are only now becoming accepted in the world of software engineering.

ADP stands out from the current software landscape as a result of two unique features:

1. Its approach to quality as a continuous process

2. Its far-reaching emphasis on automation

ADP can be applied to any team, regardless of its structure, projects, or development method. ADP has six basic principles:

1. Establish an infrastructure that integrates people and technology.

2. Apply best practices to avert common problems.

3. Customize best practices to meet project-specific needs.

4. Measure and track project status for informed management decisions.

5. Automate repetitive tasks.

6. Implement ADP's practices and policies incrementally.

We will look at each of these principles in detail a little later on. But first, we need to explain a few key concepts.

The Right Way and the Wrong Way to Measure Quality

You cannot get to good software unless you think about quality the right way, and you cannot think the right way if you do not have the right language to form your concepts. Too many IT managers think of a "defect" as being the same thing as a "software bug," that is, something broken in the program. They view the role of the Quality Assurance group to be to find and report bugs for the development team to fix.

This is wrong for two reasons. It is the wrong understanding of what a defect is, and it is the wrong role for QA.

As opposed to most IT managers, when I say *defect,* I do not mean only "bug," I mean anything produced by the development team that is less than good.

A defect might be in the code, or it might be in the requirements document, or in the design models or in the tests. A defect *might* be a bug—or it might be an oversight, an inconsistency, or a sloppily defined requirement.

Defects can originate in any of the phases of the development cycle, from requirements through design and construction, all the way to maintenance and support. If your QA team is looking for bugs and only bugs, you have a problem.

Deming Revolution Finally Comes to Software

The concept of *defect root cause analysis and prevention* originated in the manufacturing industry, in the fields of quality control and management, pioneered by W. Edwards Deming and Joseph M. Juran. This discipline is called Total Quality Management (TQM). Its application to software development was introduced by Watts S. Humphrey and gained some popularity in the 1990s. But it has not yet really taken root.

There are two reasons why TQM techniques have been slow to catch on in IT:

1. They were rejected by the software development culture. Many people within the industry doubted that effective defect prevention could be applied to IT.

2. Tools to support TQM for software did not exist.

"Production Line" Software

Many IT managers will tell you that a stable production process, such as an industrial "production line" model, is not possible in software. Without a repeatable process, TQM does not make much sense.

"How can we have repeatability when one product is always different from the next?" these IT managers say. "How can we have a production line when only one thing at a time is produced?"

The answer to this quandary requires rethinking what is meant by *production line*. Indeed, a production line in software development does exist, but not one producing multiple copies of the same product. The software production line exists in the transition of raw ideas into usable code.

Producing software does not require a traditional rigid production line of machines making machines, but rather *a sophisticated and flexible infrastructure*, capable of both adapting to minor changes within each development cycle, and adjusting to the major overhauls that occur from one release of software to another, or to a new product.

But whether traditional IT managers like it or not, change must come and is coming. Later in this chapter, I will explain the process your CIO should use to manage this change successfully.

While it used to be true that there were no good tools for automating these processes, it is no longer the case. I know, because I am the CEO of a company that makes just such tools. So the time is right, and these changes are coming.

In case you still need convincing, let's recall the story of how Deming transformed the automobile industry.

Deming versus U.S. Automakers

Manufacturing industries have learned how to create high-quality, affordable, and abundant products using defect prevention techniques. The automotive industry is a prime example of this paradigm shift. For the automotive industry, a major advance in product quality was made when the meaning of testing was redefined. In the years before World War II, automakers in the United States and Europe would test their products after they came off the assembly line. Defects would be corrected one by one.

There were two problems with this approach. First, it delayed completion and delivery of the final product, making production more expensive than it should have been. Second, it was ineffective in identifying all of the defects, allowing many faults to remain in the autos after they had been shipped to market. This led to a short product life and high consumer dissatisfaction.

After the war, this hunt-and-fix mentality remained deeply rooted in the U.S. automotive industry. Deming tried to educate the auto industry about error prevention techniques and their application to the assembly line.

When his efforts were discounted in the United States, Deming turned to the Japanese, who were quick to recognize and reap the potential profit that his methods offered.

Deming's great insight into the manufacturing process was that quality was essentially locked out of the process if defects were not considered until after the autos were assembled. For instance, finding a rattling piece of metal in a finished automobile would be nearly impossible.

Deming's Error Prevention Concept

Deming taught that fixing problems where they occur in the manufacturing process not only eliminates many quality problems in the finished product, but also promotes the ultimate goal of process improvement. He found that by fixing the process itself, it was possible to prevent the same types of errors from reoccurring.

Deming advocated process improvement through a root cause analysis and prevention. The basic procedure for implementing Deming's process quality improvements is as follows:

1. Identify a defect.

2. Find the root cause of the defect.

3. Locate the point in the production line that caused the defect.

4. Implement preventative practices to ensure that similar defects do not reoccur.

5. Monitor the process to verify effectiveness of the preventative practices.

For example, say inspectors on an auto assembly line discover that seat bolts are loose. The cause of this defect is that the bolts do not exactly fit the tool used to tighten them. They locate the point in the assembly line where the bolts are being tightened, and apply a corrective action by providing a tool that fits properly. Monitoring the process is accomplished by closely inspecting the seat bolts for tightness and collecting the data about the amount of time saved by using the right tool.

Once you grasp these concepts, they seem obvious. But you may be surprised to learn that they are not universally adopted in software development. In the software industry, postproduction testing is still the norm, as it was in manufacturing *more than 60 years ago*.

And postproduction testing fails in the software industry for the same reasons it used to fail in the auto industry. Looking for one fatal runtime error in 50,000 lines of code is much more difficult than looking for the same error in only 500 lines.

An Ounce of Prevention Is Worth 16 Tons of Cure

Defect prevention is not the same as defect detection. Defect detection is the process of finding and fixing defects after a product is built; the flawed process that generated those defects is left uncorrected.

In the seat bolts example, defect detection would have simply tightened the seat bolts at the end of the assembly line. This action might have ensured that the bolts were installed properly, but it would have left the root of the problem embedded in the manufacturing process. The problem would never go away because the root cause was not corrected.

Implementing Deming's methodology took time—years, in some instances—as every step in the manufacturing process had to be analyzed and, in most cases, altered. However, in adopting Deming's defect prevention techniques, Japan, Germany, and other nations saw the quality of their products skyrocket. In turn, the manufacturing process became more efficient, resulting in greater production numbers and reduction of per-unit costs.

The American automotive industry remained skeptical of the Deming approach, despite the unexpected and astonishing quality improvement experienced by the Japanese. Postproduction testing remained the standard approach to quality in the American auto industry well into the 1970s.

Only after the 1973 oil crisis, when the customers turned to smaller foreign imports in an effort to save fuel, did the American auto industry take notice. What they saw was an ever-widening gap between the quality of Japanese and European cars and their domestic counterparts. Failure to prevent defects in the production process nearly destroyed the American automotive industry altogether.

A Jumble of Nuts and Bolts

When I think of how software is produced today, in many cases it is as if there were assembly lines that produce bolts and nuts and washers and girders. To build anything useful, you need to assemble all these things together. But the manufacturing processes are haphazard and standards are few. So every nut and bolt that comes off the assembly line is a different size—and the only way to tell if a nut fits on a bolt is by trial and error!

The only reasonable way to fix this problem is to overhaul the assembly line so that you know exactly what size nut or bolt you are making and that it will be properly manufactured.

Find the Cause at the Root

Traditionally, *defect prevention* refers to identifying *root causes* of defects in a software life cycle and *preventing them from recurring.* It involves collecting defect data in a defect repository, analyzing and identifying the root causes of the most severe defects, and applying a systematic methodology to improve the software development process in order to prevent these defects from recurring.

Your team should be trained to "concentrate on vital few and not trivial many" defects. For example, once a vital defect such as a "dangling pointer" has been detected in a code module, this defect needs to be corrected, and a process should be established to prevent any future "dangling pointers" in the code.

Root causes might originate in methods, technology, or people. Once the root cause of the problem has been determined, action must be taken to prevent it from recurring. Finding the root cause of a defect often allows for fixing a whole class of defects. The entire system, therefore, becomes more stable and attains a higher level of quality.

The focus is always on improving the process, not merely repairing the defect.

Some people dismiss this approach as both costly and impractical for software. Developers and IT managers may tell you that "patching up" bugs without identifying their root causes is faster and more efficient than going to all the bother of root-cause analysis.

Do not listen to them. The ad-hoc, one-bug-at-a-time approach provides only a short-term solution, like welding the spare tire to the axle.

A Tragic Example

During the Gulf War, an American Patriot missile battery failed because of a software error that allowed aiming inaccuracies to build up over time. In training, the systems were restarted every few hours.

But in actual combat, the Patriot missile battery in Dharan, Saudi Arabia, had been running for 100 consecutive hours when it failed to intercept an incoming Iraqi Scud missile. The missile killed 28 American soldiers and wounded approximately 100.

Later analysis showed that the error had been detected and fixed in some parts of the code. But because there had been no root-cause analysis, there was no system-wide search for similar problems. And the results were tragic.

Pay Me Now, or Pay Me a Lot More Later

As with any manufactured thing, the cost of removing defects from software grows dramatically as a function of time. The later in the development cycle that you find and fix a problem, the more it costs you. Whether you are building a car or a house or a computer program, the later in the game that you find big problems, the harder it is to fix them.

Defect prevention not only reduces the total number of faults, but it also shifts defect discovery to early phases of the development cycle. Defects uncovered in one iteration of software development are prevented from recurring in subsequent iterations. This saves you time and money.

Now that I've convinced you, I hope, that ADP is the way to go, let's take a closer look at the six principles of ADP that I introduced earlier.

Role of Top Management

The CEO and other top managers should look at ADP in the same way that they now look at Deming and TQM methods. ADP is as important for software as these methods are for manufacturing.

There are several barriers that need to be overcome in order to apply TQM techniques in the software industry. The first is that IT organizations are typically structured incorrectly, with QA separate from development—typically as a process that starts only after development completes.

This does not follow what Deming recommends and other manufacturing industries practice: You never separate the responsibility for production (development) from the responsibility of verifying what is produced (QA).

As long as you stick to the traditional IT structure, with QA starting where development ends, you will continue to suffer from the same problems that automobile manufacturing had in the 1970s—when they produced cars and had QA departments at the end of production lines, trying to fix defects as cars came off the ramp.

Automakers learned that to improve quality, they needed to put testing equipment on the production line so that production would overlap with verification of the items being produced. IT must learn the same lesson.

That is to say, your processes must overlap verification of code with creation of code. Within IT, this verification is accomplished through a regression test suite. This test suite serves the same purpose as the production line testing equipment that verifies whether the items on the production line actually adhere to the appropriate standards.

With regression testing, a set of tests that actually verifies the functionality of the application is run automatically. The results of the current test run are compared with the results from the previous run. Any discrepancies here indicate that the most recent modifications have altered or broken something.

The Test Suite Is Part of the Product

A related problem is that in IT, managers often do not consider this regression test suite—the code that verifies the application—to be as essential as the code written to implement the functionality. To put Deming's findings into practice and to really overlap QA with development, you need to recognize that the application consists of two parts: the part that implements functionality and the part that verifies it.

Applications need to be designed and constructed in this way, which means that the organization must dedicate appropriate time and resources for this—just as manufacturing organizations have to invest in placing testing equipment along the production line.

Automate, Automate, Automate

There is no way to implement continuous quality (enabled by the continuous regression test suite) without automation. It is simply too expensive to have someone manually rerun regression tests by hand every day—just as it is not feasible to constantly repeat manual inspections and tests along the production line.

Automation is achieved through an integrated infrastructure. ADP Principle 1—*Establish an infrastructure that integrates people and technology*—sets the baseline that allows us to have an infrastructure. This infrastructure needs to be automated, which leads to ADP Principle 5: *Automate repetitive tasks*.

Insist on Standards

What IT needs to learn from manufacturing is the importance of standards. The manufacturing industry uses standards because they have learned that standards reduce defects by ensuring that the different pieces are built to spec, which in turn ensures that they fit together properly. That's why we have ADP Principles 2 and 3: *Apply best practices to avert common problems* and *Customize best practices to meet project-specific needs*. These both speak to the enforcement of standards.

When you proactively prevent problems by adhering to standards, there are certain things that you do not even need to test for, so you can really reduce testing time.

Deming took this one step further, into root cause analysis. To do this in IT, you need a process and an infrastructure that can be modified to correct the root causes of the problem. That is why we have ADP Principle 4: *Customize best practices to meet project-specific needs.*

Which Kind of CEO Do You Want to Be?

There is an important lesson for CEOs here. In the 1970s, top management at General Motors (GM) and other automobile manufacturers believed that they were producing the best car they could at the time. Many of today's top IT managers have this same mind-set today: They think their organizations are producing the best software they can.

As a result, they are reluctant to invest in improving the infrastructure and the process. However, Toyota executives realized that if they invested in improving their production lines, they would see improvements in market share. Roll forward 30 years, and you see the result: Toyota captured a significant market share, which GM lost. The lesson is the same. If you do not adapt, you will be left behind.

If you do what ADP recommends, you actually improve productivity. First, you overlap QA with development. Say your QA usually lasts four months after development; if QA overlaps with your development phase, you save on four months of QA payroll.

Second, you put standards in place, which relieves you from the need to do a great deal of testing, and saves you money.

There is another benefit, too: Developers become more innovative and more creative, which leads to higher quality.

Improve Quality by Improving Productivity

Remember, if you want to improve quality, you need to focus on productivity. You need to determine how to automate and thus remove repetitive and mundane tasks so that people can work smarter as well as faster. People perform mundane, repetitive tasks poorly but excel at creative ones. In fact, most of the mistakes people make are with repetitive tasks. By automating such tasks, you improve quality.

Managers often push quality initiatives without really considering how they affect productivity. They take for granted that quality increases productivity, but that is usually not the case.

If you want to introduce a quality initiative into the organization, you need to figure out how to do it in a way that does not disrupt the normal workflow. Otherwise, there is little chance of its resulting in a sustainable quality process. That is why initiatives like the Capability Maturity Model (CMM) and International Organization for Standardization (ISO) 9000 often fail: They create too much extra work and, as a result, they are rejected.

If you implement ADP, you actually get very high levels of CMM and ISO just by implementing commonsense procedures. It is very similar to normal manufacturing. People focus on increasing productivity, use automation to get more out of people on the production line, and thus improve quality.

People Matter

The process of adopting ADP, like any other process that involves people, must be a gradual one. There are no quick fixes in software development. It cannot happen overnight. It could very well take years, just as improving the production line does. It needs to be well focused and organized. That is why we have ADP Principle 6: *Implement ADP's practices and policies incrementally.* This principle suggests that we introduce it into a small group, optimize the process there, and then expand it to the rest of the organization. With this approach, you get a constant improvement in both productivity and quality.

What Kind of Productivity Improvements Are We Talking About?

The improvements in productivity are measurable. Remember, we look at the total number of LOC in the organization divided by the number of people who are working on that code, the LOC per head, as a proxy for productivity.

Currently, the industry average LOC per head is 10,000 to 20,000. This is roughly equivalent to a book of 80 pages. With ADP, I have seen productivity go up by a factor of 10, with each person responsible for between 100,000 and 200,000 lines of code—a book of about 800 pages. There are more correlations to understand in this larger volume of code, but ADP's emphasis on automation makes this possible.

When you achieve this 10× boost in productivity that ADP can deliver, it has a dramatic impact on the enterprise. Now you can implement disposable software because you can implement new code rapidly—and be confident that it works.

With this capability, you can react quickly to market changes and requirements. You gain the ability to make strategic decisions with your IT systems, which are basically the brains of your enterprise.

That is the key to achieving the second quantum leap of productivity.

Six Principles of ADP

Principle 1: Establishment of Infrastructure

By *infrastructure* I mean a well-defined system of hardware and software tools, processes, and roles for team members to play.

Build a strong foundation through integration of people and technology.

People's roles in a software team need to be defined to include active participation in and control of defect prevention. Technology must be used both to automate best practices and to track and measure project status data.

The details of the infrastructure—how people and technology are actually organized—are beyond the scope of this book. The key thing for you to insist on, as CEO, is that such an infrastructure exists.

People—Extending Traditional Roles

Building an infrastructure involves organizing employees in a way that will promote communication, productivity, efficiency, and overall job satisfaction. Traditional roles must be extended beyond their conventional definitions to include defect prevention activities.

Technology—Minimum and More

As a minimum, a development group must have a functioning source control system, an automated build system, a problem-tracking system, and an automated reporting system. As CEO, you do not need to know exactly what each of these items is, but your CIO must.

These elements must now be integrated so they form a kind of enterprise resource planning (ERP) system for software development. Then a workflow system must be added to distribute tasks to developers and to QA. This is the key piece that connects people, processes, and machines.

Gradually, the infrastructure should be expanded to include more technology and to support other groups. The process must continuously improve and, as it does, it must incorporate more and more automation.

Processes—An Orderly Sequence of Procedures

Without process, you have only random movement or chaos. A process can be a simple statement of "this is how we generally do things." A rudimentary process is the collective wisdom of the team about how they do their work. The idea is to start with a process and continuously improve it.

Understanding Roles

Each team member in the development group needs to understand his or her role—be it developer, architect, or project manager—and how to adhere to that role. Most importantly, defining group behavior and interactions with technology ensures that the practices adopted remain ingrained and that they do not deteriorate over time.

A stable, well-understood infrastructure is the foundation upon which the other five principles rest. You cannot follow best practices if you make up new practices every day. You cannot have automation (Principle 5) without infrastructure because processes are too haphazard. You must have an orderly, repeatable process from which to start. Everything flows from that.

The Role of QA

I mentioned previously that the processes of development and QA must overlap with automated regression testing to form a continuous quality process.

Once you understand the importance of process and the continuous improvement of process, it becomes apparent that the role of QA at the tail end of the development cycle is all wrong.

In too many cases, QA and development are different teams. In the worst case, QA is tasked with verifying that products are built correctly, *after development has finished building them.*

This is like testing whether the nuts and bolts fit each other, without knowing what size they are. You do not want your QA group doing that! Of course, you do need some way to detect problems; that is what test suites and regression tests and similar techniques are for. The question is *where* and *when* they find defects.

You want to find defects in small items *as you build code*. This is the same as a normal production line—you verify quality of the item as it is being built. This is accomplished through regression testing, as taught by Deming.

But mainly, you want QA verifying that the correct process is being followed—as the product is being built, not afterwards. And you want QA working side by side with development, finding ways to improve the process.

Principle 2: Application of General Best Practices

I have already mentioned the need for standards. Standards are lessons learned from the mistakes of others.

Learn from the mistakes of others.

When teams are working on any type of project, it is always prudent to follow the practices and standards that industry experts have designed for the applications, languages, platforms, and technologies they are using. A "best practice" could be as abstract as the type of software development process selected for a project, or as concrete as conventions for naming specific variables in the code.

For example, requiring code review before any developer's work becomes part of the product is a well-established best practice. When one developer reviews another's code, he learns about code complexities and connections he would not know about otherwise.

This improves the developer's understanding of the code and increases LOC per head.

This ends up expanding the amount of code that each developer can work on, which enables the team to accomplish more with its existing resources. In addition, when a developer receives feedback on his code, he becomes a better developer.

This is not only invaluable for getting new developers up to speed rapidly, but it is also key to promoting the entire team's continued growth. With all developers engaged in this "continuing education" process, developers are accomplishing more because they are working smarter.

In fact, code review is the only genuinely effective way to find complex problems in software systems as you build them.

Principle 3: Customization of Best Practices

Some practices are very valuable in one type of development context, but not applicable to others. The team working on

Learn from your own mistakes.

embedded C software for a pacemaker has different concerns from the team developing a fast-action software game.

Even though the same core general practices apply in most cases, these core practices should be supplemented to suit each project's unique needs.

But how do you customize practices in an orderly way? The answer is based on Deming's error prevention concept. Every time a severe defect is discovered, a new customized practice should be defined. After the new practice is defined, it must become an integral part of the methodology and its application must become, if possible, automated and seamless (see Figure 4.1).

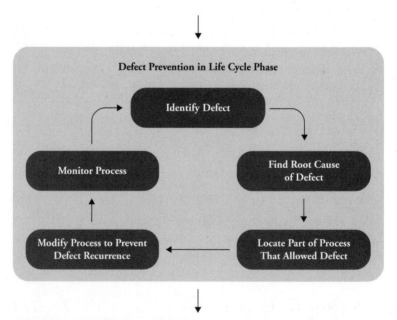

Figure 4.1 Deming's Defect Prevention Applied to a Phase in the Software Development Process

Principle 4: Measurement and Tracking of Project Status

To make informed deci-
sions, management must
be able to tell what is
really going on. To do
that, you have to mea-
sure. If your IT group

> **Understand the past and present to make decisions about the future.**

is not rigorously and objectively measuring its performance
and taking steps to improve that performance, then it is not
really being managed at all. You don't have software engineering, you have a guild. You are using nineteenth-century
approaches to twenty-first-century problems.

Tracking

The only way to assess progress and keep the project organized is to continuously track project data. For example,
the tracking of requirements helps identify their changes
and the status of their implementation. As the project stabilizes,
the number of implemented and tested requirements should
gradually increase while new requirements approach zero.

When new requirements are continuing to appear late into
the project, you are in a situation called "feature creep." To IT
personnel, this is such a well-known condition that the car-
toon *Dilbert,* by Scott Adams, even has a character called "the
Feature Creep." It is a hideous monster that makes it impossible
for Dilbert and his fellow IT workers to get their jobs done.

If you're not tracking project data, you have no way to
know whether the Feature Creep has taken up residence in
your IT department. In fact, it probably has.

Principle 5: Automation

Modern software systems are so complex that you simply cannot achieve reasonable qual-

Let the computer do it.

ity without using computers to help you track, integrate, and test the systems. Yet many IT shops continue to avoid automation, either because they think that automation software is too expensive or they think it is unnecessary, or—in more cases than you would believe—because their processes are so disorganized that automating them is virtually impossible—a sure sign of out-of-control processes.

Automation Improves Job Satisfaction and Effectiveness

Tedious tasks hurt employee morale. They cause frustration and boredom, which lead to ineffectiveness and errors. Automation of repetitive and mundane tasks allows team members to focus on more challenging and creative tasks by working in the high ends of their "competency zone."

Thus, the role of automation is not only to function as a substitute for people, but also to improve the working conditions for people. Since people are good at creating new processes, but not very good at maintaining them, automation helps to sustain existing processes and promote change.

Automation forces people to look at even the most seemingly well-known task in a different light. Just as automation can sometimes lead to an improvement in the business process, automation can allow developers to realize that some steps are unnecessary or that there is a better way of accomplishing a task.

Automation Helps Assure Organizational Standards

Automation and supporting technology help enforce organizational best practices and standards. Without automation, it is hard to make sure that team members are following the rules. In a software project of one million lines of code, there is no way to verify adherence to standards without automated help. With automation, the code base can be inspected every night while the developers are snuggled safe in their beds.

Principle 6: Incremental Change

No other business relies on continuous change through learning, adaptation, and innovation like the software business does.

> **Move carefully to minimize resistance and increase chances of success.**

But change is unsettling, and it can be overwhelming to both organizations and individuals. Change usually encounters resistance, since people tend to gravitate toward their comfort zone. While working in their comfort zone, people do not experience a great sense of accomplishment, but they do feel settled and secure.

To minimize resistance to yet another change, ADP must be introduced gradually: group by group and practice by practice. A pilot group of talented and motivated people working on an actual project should go first. When a well-esteemed team working on an important project can say, "We did it, and it's better than the old way," it makes it easy to propagate the new way of producing code.

The Real Payoff—Moving from Developer Leap to Enterprise Leap

When you achieve the 10× boost in productivity that ADP can deliver, it has a dramatic impact on the enterprise. You have achieved a quantum leap in developer productivity. Now you can create disposable software because you can implement new code rapidly—and be confident that it works. With this capability you can react quickly to market changes and requirements.

That will already be a great improvement, but much bigger improvements are still waiting to be claimed. You will be making software the right way. But will you be making the right *kind* of software?

In order to make the most of your newly efficient IT crew, you need to make sure that they are building an open system built around the concept of software "services," what we call *service-oriented architecture* (SOA).

When you properly apply the techniques I have explained in this chapter to the kind of software I am going to describe in Chapter 5, you gain the ability to make strategic decisions with your IT systems.

That is the key to achieving the second quantum leap of productivity, the *Enterprise Leap*. Unlike the Developer's Leap, which is measured in LOC per developer, the Enterprise Leap is measured using traditional business metrics with which you are probably more familiar—profitability, revenue growth, and market share.

Before we can get to that, however, we need to discuss enterprise architecture, which comes next.

Chapter 5

The SOA
Imperative

"In the world of software, integration means taking a body of code that works fine by itself and connecting it to the other existing parts of a program that have in turn been working fine. The integration point is typically where a software project hits big trouble."

—Scott Rosenberg

Executive Summary

If you've heard of service-oriented architecture (SOA), you may think of it as another three-letter acronym for the latest IT fad. You may have heard that it is a way to make your IT department more productive. But it is much more than that; it is the key to turning your IT group, and indeed your whole enterprise, into a source of constant innovation. Your competitors are adopting SOA to great advantage. If you miss the SOA boat, you will not get a second chance.

The Internet Changes Everything

In 2000, Rick Levine, Christopher Locke, Doc Searls, and David Weinberger published a book entitled *The Cluetrain Manifesto*, boldly announcing that although most corporations did not yet realize it, the Internet had already brought about "the end of business as usual."

Taking Martin Luther as their model, they nailed their "95 theses" on the virtual door. Two of their fundamental theses—numbers 1 and 6, to be precise—bear upon the whole philosophy of large-scale software development, and they form the point of departure for this chapter:

> *Thesis 1: Markets are conversations.*
>
> *Thesis 6: The Internet is enabling conversations among human beings that were simply not possible in the era of mass media.*

The point of Thesis 1 is that companies can no longer talk *at* their customers, suppliers, collaborators, and competitors. They have to talk *with* them; and those companies that don't figure out how to do this will wither and die.

The point of Thesis 6 is that the Internet has fundamentally changed the nature of conversations that companies have with their markets.

These are simple facts about how the business world now works. If your company is going to survive and thrive, it must develop an information technology (IT) infrastructure that facilitates conversations with the people and companies you deal with.

SOA Is the New *Lingua Franca*

The Internet has been around for a while, everybody has had some degree of experience with it, and our expectations have been set by the best Web applications out there. These expectations will continue rising for the foreseeable future.

What does this mean? It means that whatever business you *think* you are in, you are really in the service business, and you are providing (and consuming) services over the Web.

Which means that like it or not, you are going to adopt a service-oriented architecture (if you haven't already), or your company is going to perish, because SOA is the language that this new marketplace speaks.

Some executives still resist the whole SOA movement, but this argument is over; the marketplace has decided. We will explain why this is in a moment, but first, come to terms with this fact: You are an SOA shop now.

In adopting SOA, your IT infrastructure is going to have to move to a model of published APIs (application program interfaces) that are used by internal and external parties over whom you have no control. Depending on how far along the adoption curve you are, this may prove to be a long, wrenching process fraught with technical, economic, managerial, and cultural obstacles.

And the return on investment, at first, may be negligible. If you are a chief information officer (CIO) proposing a big budget for moving to this new architecture and your boss wants to know what the project return on investment (ROI) is, you may have to say, "Nothing."

But wait—it gets worse.

To Gain Control You Must Give Up Control

We said that markets are conversations, and that you are going to be having conversations with customers, suppliers, partners, service providers, regulatory agencies, and even competitors using the interfaces defined in your SOA.

We have further said that you are not going to have control over these external entities. Here is the really fun part: You are going to have to give them control over you! Well, not quite. But you are going to have to open up your processes so that everybody who legitimately consumes a service that you are offering has a way to participate in the evolution of that service over time.

In other words, you are not going to be able to get away with saying, "Here's how our service works." You are also going to have to say, "Here's how our service works and here's how you can help us improve it." This is called *SOA governance*, and making sure it is done right is going to become your CIO's most important job.

To summarize what I have told you so far:

- You have no choice but to move to SOA.

- You will be glad you did, because when you do it right, it will make your enterprise fabulously successful.

And all that you are going to have to do to move to SOA is to change your IT philosophy, your software development methodology, and your corporate culture.

And I haven't even told you what SOA is yet.

What Is "an Architecture," and Why Should I Care?

People in the computer and IT fields have a way with jargon. A *cookie* is not something you eat, *boot* is not something you wear, and *architecture* has nothing to do with buildings. Usually, you can leave such jargon in the domain of the geeks (which is the jargon term that IT people use to refer to themselves).

When it comes to how your enterprise uses its IT assets, however, there are a few basic terms and concepts you must master—in particular, *architecture* and *service-oriented architecture*. Why? Because the future of your enterprise depends on how well you put them to use. SOA is not merely about how computers are structured, it is about how businesses and organizations are structured. It is going to affect everything you buy and everything you sell.

When used by geeks, the term *architecture* means the general style in which the parts hang together. That is a pretty vague definition, for sure, but it is still useful. Let me give some examples.

In the earliest days of computers, the architecture was "mainframe/datacenter"—large computers sat in special rooms where they were operated by technicians. Only these technicians interacted with the computers, each of which was an island unto itself.

As time went on, computers came out of the data centers and into people's offices, and now, even into their pockets. At first, these computers were connected to each other in discrete clumps called local area networks, and an architecture called *client/server* emerged.

In that scheme, one powerful central computer (the server) would run a program, and many less powerful computers used by individuals (clients) would access it over the local network. Individual computers could also run "shrink-wrap" software, that is, programs intended to be used on one machine only.

If you were buying software for your company to use, you would either purchase a server version with a license to use it on however many "seats," or else you would purchase as many shrinkwrap versions as you needed. But in either case, what you were buying was access to a discrete program with a discrete set of capabilities and functions.

As the Internet became more and more embedded in everyday business life and individual PCs became ever more powerful, the basic client/server + shrinkwrap model evolved, but remained pretty much intact.

Until now.

Finally, We Are Talking to Each Other

Since the introduction of the Internet, no other technology has advanced communication between disparate, heterogeneous applications and systems as SOAs have. Before the Internet, computers in different parts of the world, or even the same room, could not easily communicate with each other.

But with the advent of the Internet, computers were, for the first time, able to identify each other and transmit data to one another. However, there was still a communication barrier: Machines on different systems and applications still could not easily communicate with each other since there was no common protocol for message payloads. SOA and SOAP changed this.

SOAP, whose name originally derived from "Simple Object Access Protocol," is a way for defining the structure of objects that are passed between different programs.

Through the use of SOAP and Web services, SOA allows any computer to exchange messages with any other computer, regardless of platform, language, or development environment.

In much the same way that the Internet opened new avenues for the broad Internet, SOA has provided completely new possibilities for the communication between disparate systems. Interestingly, many of these opportunities have a very fortunate side effect: They can ultimately save businesses millions of dollars through asset reuse and business process orchestration.

SOA: Services, Not Programs

SOA is a way of producing software so that programs can be easily built, virtually on the fly, from discrete parts that reside on the Internet.

You can think of SOA as an extension of the Internet, a way to arrange your IT infrastructure to take full advantage of the Internet. So it is just as important as the Internet itself. If you are using the Internet in your company without using SOA, it is as if you were using a hammer to pound screws into wood instead of using a screwdriver.

SOA is simply a way of decomposing large applications into smaller chunks that can talk to each other over the Internet. Some of these chunks will reside on computers owned and managed by your IT group, but some of the chunks reside elsewhere on the Internet—they may belong to your supplier, customer, investor, government regulator, or whatever.

So instead of having lots of large, autonomous, self-contained applications, in SOA there are lots of services that communicate with each other in a loosely coupled way. The notion of a "program" as a discrete set of capabilities begins to fade away.

This is not a matter of trying to keep up with the Joneses; it is a matter of trying to keep up with every business in the world that has access to the Internet—because any one of them could be your competitor tomorrow.

As I am typing these words, competitive organizations everywhere are scrambling to refocus and reengineer their IT strategies around the Internet. But accomplishing this amazing feat will require massive changes in the software running throughout the IT infrastructures of all these businesses.

An Example: Shipping 'R' Us

Imagine that you are the CEO of an international shipping company; let's call it Parcel Express. You are in the business of shipping parcels around the world, and you own a giant fleet of trucks, thousands of warehouses, and hundreds of airplanes.

For any given parcel, one of your employees may need to know, at any time, who sent it, whom it is going to, what is in it, how much it weighs, who is paying for it, where it is now, and so forth. All of this information is privileged, but there are widely diverging classes of privilege.

The fellow driving the truck might need only to know where a package is going and how much it weighs. The sender might need to know where her parcel is, but she probably does not get to know the name of the truck driver responsible for it right now. And so forth.

It is not hard to imagine dozens, maybe even hundreds of entities within and without your company that would have a legitimate need to interact with data about that parcel.

SOA would essentially enable you to merge and stream-line the processes, share data fluidly, and reuse the existing software within each system.

With SOA, sales, marketing, and finance would have access to the same customer data. Operations and customer service would be able to check the status of open orders. Finance and account management would have access to credit and accounting data so they could customize their tactics for handling late-paying customers.

Of course, there is a lot more to it than that, but this is not a book for programmers, so we are not going to get too technical. Here is what you really need to know right now about SOA:

- SOA enables you to reuse the code you already have. Before SOA, you could reuse an entire system, or none of it. With SOA, you can reuse parts of the system.

- SOA allows you to expose your code in standard blocks. It is like building with a Lego set—the only limit is the creativity of the architect.

So, from the point of view of your IT department, SOA is imperative for two reasons:

1. SOA is becoming the standard language for providing (and consuming) services over the Internet. It's what allows the different players in this new marketplace to communicate with one another.

2. It improves the efficiency of IT resources, ultimately allowing you to do more with fewer people.

But here is why I think that SOA is truly amazing: It enables you to automate a much broader range of repeatable human activities. And this allows you to automate decision-making processes that do not rely on creativity.

SOA Is a Business Tool, Not Just an IT Tool

SOA is not merely about developing software. It is about seeing into how your enterprise actually works, and improving it.

When properly implemented, SOA will give you, for the first time, a true understanding of how your enterprise really works, at any level of detail. With that understanding, you can revolutionize your organization from the bottom to the top, eliminating redundancy, finding new opportunities, and institutionalizing constant innovation.

When Honda began using robots on its assembly lines, the robots would build a component and then wait for a human worker to carry the finished component to the next robot on the line. The person doing the carrying might have been an extremely creative person—but the assigned task did not require creativity.

Honda realized this, and in a subsequent iteration of their automation strategy, the person carrying finished components from one robot to another was replaced by a robot. Now there are no human workers on the production line— only supervisors.

Getting the Most from Your Assets

As I mentioned earlier, one of the business benefits driving SOA initiatives is the opportunity to reuse business components, which may be just one or several parts of a complete working system.

For example, a bank might offer a Web service that performs loan appraisals (by looking up assessor files) as just one part of its home loan system. In a pre-SOA world, this capability would be locked inside the home loan application. In an SOA world, this capability would be exposed to the world by a well-defined interface so that team members, business partners, bank regulators, and so forth, might have access to it.

Rather than having team members or partners redoing, re-creating, and rerunning the same assets over and over again,

SOA allows you to ensure that assets are created, shared, leveraged, and extended properly.

Instead of writing code, you can reuse what already exists within your organization, or use code provided by someone else. This provides huge savings by reducing the cost of development. Sometimes the best way to program is not to program at all.

And as we said, you are in a conversation with your service consumers. You cannot simply dictate terms to them; you are going to have to evolve a process in which they can participate.

The Real Payoff of SOA: Business Process Engineering

SOA makes business logic visible so that you can easily orchestrate and improve it. For example, assume that a bank's loan process involves the following workflow, which passes through a number of programs: A customer requests a loan via the Web service; this request is analyzed by a bank employee, who might in turn perform a series of appraisals, credit checks, financing, and so on.

When you convert each of these programs to a Web service, first of all, you are going to find a lot of duplicated software functionality that can now be eliminated.

In addition to discovering unnecessary software capabilities, you are going to find unnecessary tasks that *people* are doing. Said bluntly, a more streamlined process requires fewer people to run it, just as a supertanker requires fewer people to sail it than an eighteenth-century merchantman did.

Business process management (BPM) was designed to define and automate these types of Web service–enabled business processes. It allows process automation without traditional coding and programming; as a result, automated processes can be rapidly prototyped, developed, and modified—even by individuals with limited development experience.

This means that you, the CEO, can play around with ways of structuring your business just as you would play around with Legos. When you find a better way of organizing *the business,* through Web service–enabled processes and BPM, it is a relatively straightforward matter to use automated tools to create the software you need to make this new organization reality.

Governance and Evolution

Since every change you make now impacts others, a governance process is required. What does *governance process* mean? It means that you need to have regular procedures that define who can change any part of the IT infrastructure, what can and cannot be changed, and how changes are made. The process must specify as well who needs to approve each change before it is actually deployed.

In SOA, everything can potentially interact with everything else. The number of pairwise interactions between component parts is virtually limitless. That means that individual "handshakes" cannot be negotiated; there must be standards and the standards must be set correctly the first time, since changing them is so difficult and expensive. SOA unites not just different groups within an enterprise, but their suppliers, customers, governmental agencies, and the like. The people affected by an architectural decision, the stakeholders, may very well work for different organizations—different corporations.

Before, you could get away with having geeks running around and changing systems on an ad-hoc basis. Now that IT systems are more important and interconnected, such change could have a significant impact on your enterprise and beyond. There has to be a well-defined governance process that defines:

- What the interface should look like

- What each service is supposed to perform

- How each service behaves

- How changes are verified and who approves them before they are deployed

In one sense, this is not any different from any other governance process in the organization. If IT changes improperly, it will create countless headaches—just as if the organization's accounting practices were changed improperly. Fortunately, with IT, compliance with the governance process can be automated.

But in another sense, this is a whole new ballgame. Before SOA, any changes you made to your system affected only a limited number of people within your organization.

But since SOA allows communication between so many endpoints, both internally within the company and externally with business partners and customers, there are many more demands on any particular interface, and there is much more risk involved should the service fail.

We will come back to governance again in Chapter 6, as we take a closer look at the roles of the CEO and CIO as your IT group evolves.

SOA Means Openness

Any single change to one part of the SOA may affect many other parts and users of the system. To go back to our parcel shipment example, let's say your company decides to standardize on metric units of weight: no more pounds and ounces for you; from now on you are dealing strictly in grams and kilograms.

Although it might take a lot of work, you might even be able to pull it off and have all programs that interact with data converted to kilograms.

But what about your customers and suppliers? What if *they* are not prepared for the change from pounds to kilograms? The effects could be catastrophic and result in their taking their business to your competitors. Clearly, any change like that would have to involve many interested parties beyond your direct control.

That is to say, SOA provides enormous potential for cost savings, but you can lose much of the business benefits that SOA provides from reusing software assets and improving business processes if you break the code and infuriate your best customers or most important partners.

To protect your organization from these business risks, you are going to need a solid SOA governance strategy for determining how services are handled in their different life cycle stages, from inception to discovery, to invocation and consumption.

It is crucial that developers, *both internal and external*, have some sort of participation in the process for determining what services are published and become a part of the SOA.

In order to control how Web services are defined, developed, and deployed, your company will have to grow its own organic governance process. This governance process will use internal standards and policies as well as industry guidelines and best practices. These policies specify which standards are adopted within a particular organization, and which versions of these standards are endorsed.

And that governance strategy must be able to itself evolve as conditions change. SOA governance, as an overarching management activity, is going to become a fundamental responsibility of the CIO.

Managing Risk and Security

Once you move to SOA, you have opened up your IT infrastructure, to at least some degree, to your customers, suppliers, partners, investors, government regulators—and in some sense to everybody on the Internet, including criminals. SOA implies openness on a scale never before seen in IT.

But an unprecedentedly open system opens the door to unprecedented risks. Before, the system had only one interface: the user interface, which was well defined and well tested. Now, virtually anything can serve as a system interface, and any message that comes from another system could be a threat.

David Temkin, founder and chief technology officer of Laszlo Systems, creator of the OpenLaszlo rich Internet application platform, offers a good explanation of SOA and its relationship to the organization:

> *Typically, it used to be the case that if you wanted to get information from a repository, you wrote a specific application to get to it. Each application was a closed system, end to end. In an SOA model, enterprises define interfaces that allow the creation of enterprise toolboxes. These interfaces are readily exposed behind firewalls, with all the security concerns that go with that. In an information-rich company, you may have well over a thousand distinct applications that interact. As a result, system security needs to be taken very seriously. When IT systems contain all of the enterprise's data, customer information, procedures, and so on, a virtual break-in can be devastating.*

Blithely assuming that IT is capable of handling security risks is itself a huge risk. To be safe, you need to actively ensure that IT has real security policies and can satisfactorily define how these policies protect the new open system architecture.

Getting Ready to Put It All Together

Gary Beach, publisher emeritus of *CIO* magazine, made an interesting remark about SOA during a recent interview:

> *Last year people were making fun of SOA, saying it stood for "Seriously Over Advertised." Now they're talking about SOA as a way to grow their businesses.*

I think that Beach is correct. And now let's take it a step further.

Because SOA is a market imperative, because SOA implies openness, because security and risk management are becoming even more important and challenging than they were pre-SOA, and because SOA, when properly combined with disposable software, offers you the opportunity of a lifetime to meet and exceed your organization's goals, top managers will have to look long and hard at their IT organizations—and at their CIOs—to make sure that they are up to the tasks ahead.

You will need to make sure they have the right skills, right attitudes, and right incentives to enable the Enterprise Leap in productivity. In the final chapter, I will tell you how to do that.

Chapter 6

Achieving a Quantum Leap in Enterprise Productivity

"Probably never before has a theory been evolved which has given a key to the interpretation and calculation of such a heterogeneous group of phenomena of experience as has quantum theory."

—Albert Einstein

Executive Summary

You can propel your enterprise to ever-greater levels of productivity and success by turning your information technology resources into engines of innovation and creativity. But first, you may have to change the whole culture of your IT group from "playing it safe" to "leading the way." Bringing about this cultural transformation is perhaps the trickiest part of the whole process. It is your job to make sure it's done right.

Unleashing the Power of Productivity
Is *Your* Job

In the preceding five chapters, I explained how new and
better IT strategies make possible new and better business
strategies. By improving software development practices to
automatically prevent defects, and by structuring all enterprise projects around service-oriented architecture (SOA),
you position your enterprise for success.

By adopting the proper information technology (IT) governance model, you further enhance your chances of making
a quantum leap in enterprise productivity. Making the most
of this work is up to you, however. In other words, the IT
group must do everything it can to get ready for your leadership, but the chief executive officer (CEO) retains responsibility for transforming the entire enterprise to make the most
of this new strategic asset.

Unlocking of productivity happens by changing two things
at once. First, IT has to change itself by becoming more nimble, responsive, and productive. It does so by applying the
tried-and-true principles of Total Quality Management (TQM)
to software development. That is how IT improves its productivity and achieves the first quantum leap.

135

Equally important, you have to change how you view and use IT. If you continue to think of IT as a utility, a sunk cost, you will never keep up with the leaders in your industry. Industry leaders realize that IT is a strategic asset, a tool for creating change and innovation. They budget it that way, they staff it that way, and they manage it that way.

As your IT group adopts the six principles of Automated Defect Prevention (ADP), its productivity will greatly improve. You must be able to understand and verify that this happened.

Over this transitional period you should be working closely with your chief information officer (CIO), and making a cool-headed assessment of whether you have the right person for the job. You will be forging a partnership with the CIO, so you had better make sure that you have an excellent person in that spot. If you do not have the right person, however painful it may be, you must make a change.

As ADP and SOA become established, the CIO increasingly becomes a resource for ideas about how to improve productivity of the enterprise. I repeat: The CIO becomes a key player in finding ways to improve the productivity of the entire enterprise, not merely the IT domain.

This leads to the second quantum leap in productivity, which is at the enterprise level. It is achieved by gluing current human processes with computer programs, by finding new and unexpected sources for creating new products and expanding market share, and by responding more quickly to new opportunities than any of your competitors can.

The Unexpected Gift of Sarbanes–Oxley

The Sarbanes-Oxley Act of 2002 (SOX) requires all publicly traded companies in the United States to provide extensive financial information to regulatory agencies. Recent rulings by the Securities and Exchange Commission further stipulate that the information be provided in a uniform manner; in fact, the information must be provided in SOA-friendly Extensible Markup Language (XML) format.

People will argue the costs and benefits of SOX for as long as the earth turns, just as they argue over the costs and benefits of taxes. Some people will say SOX is good because it makes it easier for investors to see what is really going on inside a corporation; others will say SOX is bad because it adds unnecessary layers of complexity to corporate operations.

I am here to say that SOX is a boon to the corporations!

The SOX reporting requirement, which may seem onerous or unwarranted or intrusive or whatever bad thing you want to say, is actually a blessing in disguise. Because the only reasonable way to gather and report that information on a regular basis is to have a well-functioning IT group that can produce this kind of information in virtually any format at the drop of a hat.

If your IT group cannot do that, you are in trouble. And you should be grateful to SOX for bringing the problem to your attention.

SOX forces your IT group to become an agent for transparency and to behave transparently. Vast improvements in productivity are virtually at your fingertips.

There is no point in complaining about SOX; it is not going to go away. Rather, you should embrace it as a forcing function to bring your IT group up to the next level of productivity. Instead of stopping when you get to SOX compliance, go the rest of the way to a fully functional SOA shop.

Here is why: SOX requires the business to define processes and to define the steps within the processes. Now the CIO can follow SOX processes, which are themselves business processes spanning multiple IT systems. The CIO can use SOX as a road map for figuring out which processes can be automated with business process management (BPM).

What this really means is that SOX, by forcing compliance, lays the groundwork for the automation of business processes. This automation greatly enhances productivity.

But all this means that you need the right IT governance model and the right CIO.

Fundamental Paradox of IT Process Improvement

If I were to write what I have stated in this book so far as an equation, it might look something like this:

Developer Leap in productivity + SOA + Correct IT Governance = Potential Enterprise Leap in productivity

Notice the word *potential* in the above equation. What I am trying to get across here is that even if your CIO and your IT group do everything right ("right" according to the Book of Kolawa, that is!), there is still no guarantee that you will see the kind of productivity gains that you should.

That is because it is up to you, the CEO, and to the rest of the organization, to make sure that your brand-new, highly productive IT engine is put to good use. So a good place to start is to make sure that you really understand that equation.

We have already covered the Developer Leap in productivity and SOA in some depth, but I think we need to take a closer look at what I mean by "correct IT governance."

After all, I have said that ensuring correct IT governance will become the CIO's most important job. This is a tricky assignment that requires a rare combination of technical savvy and leadership skills.

Correct IT governance requires managing the natural tension between adhering to standards and allowing for creativity. It requires absolute enforcement of the rules, while creating a climate in which people can come up with new and better ways to do things and create *new* rules.

In Chapter 4, I explained that ADP is what geeks might call *locally rigorous software engineering practice*, where "local" just means that the concepts are applied to small teams, not to the organization as a whole, and "rigorous" means that you cannot avoid it. In that chapter, I stressed the importance of automation. As the process becomes more and more refined, it becomes more and more automated.

In fact, the six principles of ADP, in a way, are a mechanism for making the software process inescapable. The process, when properly automated, reduces the freedom of individual engineers.

Before, it might have been possible for individual developers to ignore standards and guidelines. Now computers enforce those guidelines and standards. If a developer's code does not follow the rules, it is literally impossible for him to add it to the system.

So it would seem that to make this system work, you will have to recruit and retain the kind of IT personnel who are willing to live by the rules, who do not feel the need to put their own personal style on every bit of code they write. And you are going to need managers who are good at enforcing the law.

But in Chapter 5, I said that your processes must be open, that you cannot dictate terms, and that your customers, partners, suppliers, and so forth, are going to demand an active role in developing and changing your processes. For this kind of system to work, you are going to need senior managers who are not overly controlling, and who are open to change and participatory decision making. This would seem like a contradiction. We need more control and less control at the same time!

I think it is more helpful to look at this situation not as a contradiction, but as an unavoidable tension in any dynamic system. And a natural tension can be a very good thing. Let's see how.

The *New World* Is More Complicated than the *Old World*

Service-oriented architectures are "open" by their very nature. Once the systems are set up, your firm's computers are talking to computers of your suppliers, investors, employees, customers, governmental regulators, and, alas, mischief makers and criminals—all without explicit human intervention.

As the business model becomes more complex and more dynamic, the burden on IT increases. Increasingly complex business models that depend on multiple business partners to deliver goods and services across multiple channels only add to the burden. Clearly, this system cannot work unless there are very clear rules for exchanging information and very strong protections to keep the bad guys out.

That is why IT governance is so important. Governance is comprised of two things: making the rules and enforcing the rules.

This task is never done.

This Is Not *Deadwood*

The HBO television series *Deadwood* takes place in a nearly lawless gold-rush town on the American frontier in the late 1800s. Without an effective governance policy, your IT infrastructure under SOA may come to resemble that kind of place. But when you put the right policies in place, you have happy citizens, and the gold just piles up.

Policies and approaches to SOA governance must arise organically in the organizations they serve, and each organization is different. You are going to have to grow your own. But I can tell you the elements that are going to have to be in place for an effective governance strategy over the long term. These elements include

- Appropriate scale

- Definition of scope

- Clear communication of rules

- Separation of architectural and business issues

- Documentation of rationales

- Opportunity to participate

- Strong enforcement

- Ability to evolve

All aspects of your SOA governance must be appropriately scaled to the problem they address.

Municipal laws and regulations apply to issues such as which side of the street I can park on, and whether we should put that new addition on the high school. Federal laws concern treaties among nations.

Your SOA governance is like that. It must handle issues from the local, which might apply to coding standards or peer review methods at the team level, to the global, such as whether your infrastructure will standardize on a common protocol, such as Simple Object Access Protocol (SOAP).

Every portion of the SOA governance must be clear about what domain it applies to. Some portions of SOA policy will apply to individual developers, and some will apply to managers of large functional areas, or to CIOs.

In order to play by the rules, people need to know what the rules are. Therefore, your CIO must make a concerted effort to ensure that everybody knows the rules and the processes by which rules are decided and enforced. It is not sufficient to have a policy book that explains "how we do software here." You must make a continuous effort to educate your community.

All stakeholders must have at least some way to participate in the process at the appropriate level. That does not mean that your company or enterprise is now a democracy, or that everyone who thinks he or she is an expert is entitled to a seat on a review board.

But your processes must be open and participatory to at least some extent. Not because you feel like being generous and welcoming, but because you need to capture as much of the community's wisdom as you can, and because your competitors are certainly opening up their processes and giving your customers a greater chance to control their own destiny.

Philip J. Windley, in a great article on SOA governance in *Information Week,* wrote:

> *Building codes would not be very effective at creating safe, pleasant cities if there were no building inspectors. Similarly, SOA policies aren't worth anything unless they're enforced."*

Now you see why I said that managing SOA and IT governance is going to be your CIO's most important job. The process must generate rules that are understood and accepted by everybody, but which are subject to continuous evaluation and improvement. The CIO must make sure that this process is set up and smoothly running, but he or she cannot control it.

The process thus becomes not just a way to make rules and enforce them, but also a way to harness all the creativity of everybody using the system, even people who do not work for you. A properly governed SOA allows you to leverage all your in-house IT assets, as well as all those who are connected to it. The computing power at your disposal just went up immeasurably.

What Does the Enterprise Leap in Productivity Look Like?

The Enterprise Leap in productivity can be measured not in IT quantities such as "lines of code per head," but in traditional business metrics such as revenue growth, market share, and profitability. It may be hard to capture an exact return on investment (ROI) from making the investments in IT that I am advocating in this book, because if you follow my advice to its logical conclusion, you will be transforming your entire organization, not merely IT. The returns on investment will be widely spread.

Let's imagine some scenarios of what that might look like.

Say you are a manufacturing concern with plants in 12 U.S. states, two countries in Europe, and one in South America. Imagine that you have warehouses and a fleet of trucks, and that a third of your customers are in the Far East.

Before SOA, each plant probably had its own applications that kept track of operations, its own small IT group, and a plant comptroller in charge of collecting financial information and rolling it up to corporate headquarters in the appropriate format. Switching manufacturing loads from one plant to another was a subjective process involving a lot of guesswork and politics.

With SOA, you can model all the activities going on in all your operational sites. Using BPM, you can examine entirely new ways of organizing the workflow by simulating Web service–enabled processes. When you find one you like, the optimized workflow can be rapidly deployed via Business Process Execution Language (BPEL) or other BPM automation technologies. You may find that computers can now allocate resources better than people can—at a fraction of the cost.

Because you have well-defined interfaces that are endorsed by your partners and suppliers, you now get the benefit of *their* SOA applications, which are looking for ways to get more business from you.

You can see immediately which work can be outsourced and which IT groups are redundant. Your partners show you how much you can save by getting out of the logistics and trucking business and handing all of that work to a third party that specializes in warehousing and trucking. Suddenly you have found ways to cut costs, get products to market faster, and eliminate unproductive politicking.

Your bottom line shows benefits from getting out of the trucking business, from moving production closer to the market it serves, from better scheduling, and so forth. Are they IT leaps in productivity? No, not really. These are all Enterprise Leaps in productivity. But they would have been impossible without ADP, SOA, and an effective governance process.

Tasks and Decision Points

I find it helpful to think of the work of any enterprise as a large collection of tasks. Each of these tasks can be done by a person or by a machine. Some tasks are physical, of course, such as assembling cars or building walls. But some tasks are merely the making of a decision (after gathering and analyzing all pertinent information, naturally).

Achieving the Enterprise Leap in productivity, then, is a matter of regularizing these tasks, automating them wherever possible, and using the freed-up resources to create new opportunities.

With SOA and BPM, it becomes possible to recognize and regularize tasks that are simply decision points. You will find that many of these decision points, once they have been properly modeled in software, no longer require a human agent. You can get the human out of the picture, which will reduce labor costs and increase speed at the same time.

Your goal is to find all decisions that can be made by a machine and turn them over to the machines. Save your human assets for decisions that really require human smarts and creativity. This makes the most of both your physical and human capital.

Consider the simple example of processing loan applications. Say you own a bank and your policy is that every loan application below $5,000 is basically accepted. You do not need a person to review each and every application. A computer looks at all the applications and automatically approves any requests below $5,000.

Similarly, if the loan amount is above $5,000 but below $50,000, your algorithm now says that if the applicant has a FICO credit score of 700 or above, the application is accepted, and if it is below 600, it is rejected.

Here again, the computer can accept or reject the loan for you; no person is needed. Only if the applicant's credit score is between 600 and 700 do you require a loan officer to make a subjective evaluation and render a decision. Since a machine can decide every loan below the $5,000 threshold or above the FICO 700 threshold, you need a person only for the cases that fall in the gray area in the middle.

The cost savings and efficiencies of this approach are obvious. Loan applications that used to take weeks and cost hundreds of dollars to process now take 15 seconds and are done over the Internet.

I realize that the above example is trivial; you might even say it is obvious. But it only seems obvious because we have gotten used to loan applications being made that way.

I am hereby promising you that when you implement SOA and BPM, you will find many tasks in your own business that are exactly analogous to the bank loan processing example. When you break down tasks into a series of decision points, you will quickly see which of those decisions can be safely and profitably handed over to machines.

Tasks that once seemed unique and nonrepeatable will become regularized. And then the next step is obvious: automate, automate, automate.

What Should You Look for in a CIO?

It should be clear that spearheading major change is not an easy task. As a group, CIOs are famously risk averse. They know that if the system goes down, or if a hacker gets into sensitive areas, it will be bad for the corporation and maybe the end of their careers.

So CIOs tend to be a cautious breed. "Don't mess anything up" might as well be the official IT motto. But to make the kind of changes I have called for, you are going to need somebody who can see the big picture and imagine things two, three, or five years into the future.

The key here is that we are talking about a new kind of CIO, a CIO not cut from the follow-the-herd, don't-rock-the-boat cloth of the 1980s and 1990s. What this different CIO has to do is really completely understand how IT is used throughout the organization, especially paying attention to what tasks people perform in the course of their jobs. He or she needs to create an IT group that continually analyzes these tasks, ruthlessly hunting down any activities that are not actually creative (which means that they have decision points which cannot be structured).

The IT group is still concerned with technology, of course; it still needs to make sure that the network stays up and that the bad guys are kept out. But more and more the IT group is becoming the *business process analysis and automation group*. It is a whole new mind-set, starting with a whole-hearted commitment to building disposable software, and building it the right way.

To instill this mind-set throughout the IT organization, you need somebody who can lay down the law and make sure that the principles of ADP are adopted. This will require backbone because developers will resist some of these changes. Some of these changes will actually be perceived as threatening.

You need somebody who can build high morale among your best IT staff, and get rid of those who do not have what it takes, or who are no longer needed in the streamlined world of SOA.

You need somebody who can teach IT personnel that their job is not to write code, but to *solve business problems*. And finally, you need somebody who recognizes the importance of process, somebody who can let go of the reins and let the collective wisdom of IT as a whole find the best solutions to whatever problems arise.

Your IT group can become the power plant that drives your entire enterprise forward—but only if it has the right values, the right incentives, and the right leader.

An Infrastructure of Constant Creativity and Innovation

The changes I have championed in this book are guaranteed to boost the creativity of your IT staff. But most of all, they will allow *you* to unleash *your* creativity. Always keep in mind that the end goal of all of this is not to make IT more productive, it is to make *you* more productive—and the entire enterprise more nimble, responsive, and profitable.

This is a demanding undertaking. But at the end of this overhaul, your company will be able to create robust, innovative software quickly and predictably. Your software engineers and IT staff will be productive and happy; in fact, all of your employees will be having fun and creating value instead of wasting their time on repetitive chores.

Your customers and partners will be happier because your organization will be more productive and more responsive. And you—whether you are the CEO, the chief operating officer, the chief financial officer, or any other top executive—will be happy, too, because the leap in productivity you achieve will be accompanied by a leap in profitability.

Q.E.D.

Let the Artisans Stick to Cheese and Microbrews

*By John Sundman**

The techniques outlined by Adam Kolawa in this book are not entirely novel. The idea of creating reusable blocks of software recalls the late eighteenth and early nineteenth centuries, in which the basic concept of using standardized, interchangeable parts in a repeatable assembly process became the foundational element of the Industrial Revolution. The quality management techniques he is promoting have been applied in other domains, notably automobile manufacturing, since the mid-twentieth century.

But if you take the time to internalize his points about applying quality management techniques to software, about the importance of service-oriented architecture (SOA) and about the central role of information technology (IT) governance,

---

*John Sundman is a 30-year veteran of the software industry. He's worked at large and small companies in both Silicon Valley and Boston's fabled Route 128 corridor. His novel *Acts of the Apostles* (Vineyard Haven, MA: Rosalita Associates, 1999) is considered a geek underground classic.

you will truly have taken a first step toward achieving a giant leap. To this I would only add, your job will be a little easier and a lot more fun.

Basically, Adam says that it is high time for software developers to leave the world of artisans and join the rest of us in the twenty-first century. Don't cry for the artisans—as long as there is a taste for microbrews, handmade jewelry, and really excellent cheeses made in small batches, there will be jobs for artisans. But let's not stake the future of IT on them.

As its title suggests, *The Next Leap in Productivity: What Top Managers Really Need to Know About IT* is written primarily for CEOs, CIOs, and other senior executives. But I would like to comment on the book from the point of view of the people who stand to be most affected when a company implements the changes outlined in this book.

Who are these people? They are the technical staff, which includes software engineers, quality assurance engineers, support technicians, systems analysts, technical writers, and everybody else who keeps your IT function running.

If you are going to effectively lead these people and not merely direct them, it would be helpful if you learned to see the world through their eyes.

As a class, IT people are justifiably proud of their mastery of arcane technology that has wonderful power. And yet, unlike, say, doctors or scientists, they are also used to being ridiculed as socially inept losers. They are called *geeks* and *nerds* and *propeller-heads*. In reaction to this, they have defiantly adopted the epithet "geek" as a badge of honor.

They understand and embrace their heritage, and they have a nuanced aesthetic. This is Geek Pride, and once you have understood and begun adopting Dr. Kolawa's techniques for managing IT, you will be entitled to some Geek Pride of your own.

Making Geek Pride Work for You

I have spent a good chunk of my working career down in the trenches with the technical staff. In other words, I am a geek. I have been an individual contributor, a team leader, an engineering manager of a large bicoastal group, a director of information architecture, and the chair of the software development architecture team for a large computer manufacturer whose software is used by millions of people around the world.

In my experience, a radical overhaul of practices and policies, not to mention of systems architecture, such as Adam lays out in *The Next Leap in Productivity* is bound to fail unless the technical staff buys into it.

So the question is this: Will your technical staff buy into the program described in this book?

My answer is an unequivocal "yes." They will buy in because it will make their jobs more satisfying and their resumes stronger. They will buy in because Adam's program is consistent with geek aesthetics and core values, and it raises their street value at the same time.

Although the ideas in this book might threaten cowboy programmers who are used to doing things their own way, serious IT professionals will welcome them.

People do not become software engineers because they like looking at computer screens all day. They do not do it because they are antisocial, or socially incompetent, or because they think in ones and zeroes. And generally speaking, they do not do it to become rich.

People go into software engineering for the same reasons that people go into all kinds of engineering—because they like solving hard problems. And they like solving them elegantly.

Software engineering, as opposed to, say, chemical or civil engineering, has the additional benefits (from a geek's point of view) of being delightfully abstract, and providing nearly instant gratification. When you finish writing a block of code and press the button to compile it, you find out right away whether it holds together.

All good engineers feel a little dirty when they have to resort to a kludge (an ad-hoc and not elegant solution) to get a job done. They talk derisively about sloppy, inefficient programs. "Spaghetti code," they call it. Or "garbage code." They will resort to it if they have to, but they will not be happy about it.

What they value, on the other hand, is "clean code." Check out the computer section of your favorite online bookstore and see how many of the most popular books are about writing clean code or elegant code.

Read any of the popular software development blogs and see what brings out the most passion. Elegant programming, that's what. Just as mathematicians find beauty in equations and formulas and transformations, programmers find beauty in programming done right. And they strive for it.

This passion for engineering excellence is a great and generally untapped asset. Adam, in this book, is telling you how to harness that passion for the benefit of the entire enterprise.

Good software engineers do not want to waste their time tracking down bugs that could have been found by a dumb computer. Good engineers do not enjoy figuring out why the "build system" that worked yesterday does not work today.

And good engineers do not enjoy fixing the same damn bug they fixed last week, but which cropped up again when some parameter varied slightly. When engineers follow the techniques of automatic defect prevention, they do not have to spend their time on those kinds of tedious, annoying tasks.

A whole class of irritating problems goes away under Adam's regimen. And that leaves more time for IT people to concentrate on the truly interesting problems, the kind of problems that make geeks want to come to work in the morning.

Extremely Agile Adam Programming

There is a tension in the IT/programmer/software engineering world between the "rigorous process" people like Adam, and the proponents of a development philosophy called variously *eXtreme programming* (XP) or *agile development*. It is worth noting that while some critics dismiss the "agile movement" as a fad, no less a software eminence than Google, Inc. has vociferously embraced it.

The XP movement arose out of a sense of frustration with traditional software development methodologies for collecting requirements and organizing teams. Basically, it is a reaction to overly bureaucratic software organization and project management.

The XP movement has been very influential, with dozens of bestselling books having been written on the topic, and many developer conferences held. The founders of the movement include some well-known theorists of software development, and they codified their thinking in the "Manifesto for Agile Software Development," which appears on their web site (http://agilemanifesto.org). Here's the text from the provocative first page of that site:

We are uncovering better ways of developing software by doing it and helping others do it. Through this work we have come to value:

Individuals and interactions over processes and tools
Working software over comprehensive documentation
Customer collaboration over contract negotiation
Responding to change over following a plan
That is, while there is value in the items on
the right, we value the items on the left more.

Now, if you have read *The Next Leap in Productivity* atten-
tively, you will notice a rather profound point of disagreement
right off the bat between Adam and the signers of the Agile
Manifesto. The Agile Manifesto values individuals and interactions over processes and tools, and with Kolawa, it is exactly
opposite. This is a matter of emphasis, not of exclusivity.

I will not deny, however, that the points of departure
are different. "Extreme programming" is a very hot, highly
buzzed topic. Adam might appear to be an XP skeptic, somebody throwing a bucket of cold water on the hype. Is he
really claiming to be more of an expert than Google?

No. I do not see any major contradictions between the
Kolawa approach and XP. To my mind, at least, the phi-
losophies seem complementary. The bottom line is that
Automated Defect Prevention (ADP) is a basic concept that
works on infrastructure. XP programming needs this infrastructure as much as any other style of programming. In fact,
the infrastructure makes XP and agile programming possible.

The XP people favor a very lightweight process. In fact,
unit testing and code review are the only required techniques. Their message is aimed at individuals and small

teams. They are kind of anticorporate, in the sense that they seem to radiate an intense pride in their ability to do good work without all kinds of specifications, plans, and schedule reviews, which are implicitly considered corporate bloat.

Adam does not come down on the side of either lightweight or heavyweight processes. Rather, he says that when you have a process, you must continuously optimize it, improve it, enforce it, automate it. So XP is a process that needs to be automated and optimized the same way as other development processes.

Adam is a great believer in software automation. He is more than a believer—he is nearly fanatic about it. Nevertheless, there are many complex tasks of software management that are just not suitable to automation, and that is where human judgment and local policies and procedures come in.

I can imagine him saying, "Sure, use XP if you wish, at the team level. But for real productivity at the corporate level, you need to do what I'm saying." And he has facts and figures to back up his arguments.

The Opposite of Process Is Not Agility; It's a Bad Day at the Office—Lots of Them

To the extent that Adam and the XP philosophy are in conflict, I come down squarely in Adam's camp. I believe in orderly process, and I have a short story from years ago to illustrate why I feel as strongly as I do.

About 20 years ago, a leading manufacturer of UNIX computers had a problem. They had introduced a new hardware architecture and needed to update the operating system to support it. At the same time, the basic flavor of UNIX "underneath the hood" was being swapped.

It was an ambitious project, but the company had already pulled off several projects of the same apparent complexity, and confidence was high. Several hundred highly skilled software engineers were working on it—the crème de la crème. The project was supposed to take nine or ten months. It would establish the company once and for all as the undisputed king of its market.

It took three years. It ruined careers and friendships. And it nearly sank the company.

What happened? Two words: *integration failure*. Any given individual component worked fine, but when the entire giant system was built, all kinds of unanticipated interactions arose, which gave rise to intractable bugs, which required redesign of entire subsections.

Lather, rinse, repeat. This is what software geeks call *thrashing*.

When integration problems arose, it was natural, of course, for every group to place blame on every other group. When architectural problems arose, they were handled in the manner of theatrical wrestling, with rival managers squaring off in steel-cage death matches. Organizational politics substituted for computer science and sound engineering.

After this fiasco, the company got serious about managing the software development process. This time, they learned from their mistakes, and they are a software leader today.

Whether you know it or not, your company is probably in the same situation. As Adam points out, with the arrival of SOA, everybody's architectural governance problems just got vastly more complicated. If you do not have a good process in place, and good process automation, you are sailing into a storm, as far as I'm concerned. And XP alone will not keep you afloat.

When All Projects Are Part of the Giant Project, Process Is the Key

IT architecture is never "right" or permanent. At best, a good architecture is workable and flexible. Saying that you are going to get your SOA right, once and for all, is like saying that you are going eat, once and for all. Your architecture is going to have to evolve continuously, and therefore your SOA governance framework is going to have to evolve continuously.

Of all the ingenious features of the Constitution of the United States of America, perhaps none is more ingenious than Article V, which defines the way that the Constitution itself can be modified by amendment.

Societies under a constitution that does not have the equivalent of an Article V often resort to changing the constitution the hard way—by civil war. And if your processes for governing the SOA are not subject to deliberate change by a well-defined process, you are likely to have the organizational equivalent of civil wars in your community.

If your SOA governance is perceived as being promulgated from on high, a mere series of arbitrary decrees from out-of-touch bigwigs and bureaucrats, it will be subverted and it will fail.

As CEO, you need to ensure that your process is working, understood, efficient, embraced by the community, and capable of modifying itself to adapt to changing realities. It is a task you should embrace, because it is vitally important to your success, and it is a lot of fun.

Speaking as somebody who has worked in both kinds of environments, I will choose the one with a decent process for making architectural decisions and for setting development policy.

A True Partnership at Last

Why is it that software development practices and IT policy making have kept to their antiquated ways? Why has there so often been a gulf between IT and the other competencies you manage? Part of the reason is that software and computers in general have been mystifying to people outside of IT, including senior management. And, frankly, sometimes IT has cultivated that aura of mystery because it brings with it a certain amount of insulation from the demands of other parts of the organization.

For years, CIOs and IT staff have been lectured that merely understanding technology is not sufficient. They must also understand the enterprise's goals and values and align their activities in support of them. Fair enough. But, Adam Kolawa insists, it is a two-way street. Merely understanding the enterprise's objectives and values is not enough. CEOs must understand how IT works—at least to the degree that they can direct the activities of the CIO with full competence and confidence.

But if you have read this far, you have seen that when you look at software from the perspective of traditional Total Quality Management, the necessary concepts for doing so are not that mystifying at all.

Armed with that understanding, with IT properly construed as a central powerhouse and fount of innovation, you will be ready to lead your entire enterprise to whole new realms of success.

References

Agile Manifesto: http://agilemanifesto.org/

Google Embraces Agile: www.forbes.com/2008/08/09/cio-agile-computing-tech-cio-cx_dw_0811agile.html

RECOMMENDED READING

Barlow, Mike, and Michael Minelli. *Partnering with the CIO: The Future of IT Sales Seen Through the Eyes of Key Decision Makers.* Hoboken, NJ: John Wiley & Sons, 2008.

Deming, W. Edwards. *The New Economy for Industry, Government, Education.* Cambridge, MA: MIT Center for Advanced Educational Services, 1994.

Hammer, Michael. *Beyond Reengineering: How the Process-Centered Organization Is Changing Our Work and Our Lives.* New York: HarperBusiness, 1996.

Huizinga, Dorota, and Adam Kolawa. *Automated Defect Prevention: Best Practices in Software Management.* Hoboken, NJ: John Wiley & Sons, 2007.

Juran, J. M. *Juran on Quality by Design: The New Steps for Planning Quality into Goods and Services.* New York: Free Press, 1992.

Kidder, Tracy. *The Soul of a New Machine.* New York: Little, Brown and Company, 1981.

Lutchen, Mark D. *Managing IT as a Business: A Survival Guide for CEOs.* Hoboken, NJ: John Wiley & Sons, 2004.

May, Matthew E. *The Elegant Solution: Toyota's Formula for Master Innovation.* New York: Free Press, 2007.

Rosenberg, Scott. *Dreaming in Code.* New York: Crown Publishers, 2007.

Weigers, Karl E. *More about Software Requirements: Thorny Issues and Practical Advice.* Redmond, WA: Microsoft Press, 2006.

GLOSSARY

API (application programming interface): The way that any program makes itself available to other programs. Basically, it's a list of recipes programmers use to build systems from completely separate parts.

Automated build system: A system that automatically puts together all the software parts of a system, and tests it. This may include hundreds of parts that are worked on by hundreds of people every day.

Automated reporting system: A system that reports on project quality, project readiness, team processes, and policy adherence.

BPEL (Business Process Execution Language for Web services): A language that is sort of halfway between a natural human language and a computer language. You use it to create models of how you want your business to work; it can then be turned into computer code by programmers.

Enterprise platform: An environment for running applications throughout a large, often widely distributed corporation.

LOC: Lines of "source" code, the stuff actually written by programmers before it is translated into computer codes.

Problem-tracking system: A system used to track and manage the defects and change requests reported for application.

Regression test suite: A set of tests that check whether the application is producing the expected results. To *regress* means to go backwards, so these tests make sure that even as you add new capability to a system, you do not break anything that was already working.

Requirement: The definition of a business problem that a given program must actually solve.

Requirement management system: A system used to track and manage the requirements for any project that your IT group is working on.

SaaS (Software as a Service): When an application runs on a "server" machine, typically one that the customer does not own, instead of having the application installed on his or her own computer. The customer (or "user") interacts with the service through a Web browser such as Internet Explorer.

SOA (service-oriented architecture): An open, loosely coupled software architecture that enables business processes by supporting communications between Web services, or "units of work." Companies turn to SOA to promote reuse, agility, and flexibility.

SOAP (Simple Object Access Protocol): A set of rules that allows any computer to easily communicate with another computer by exchanging messages in a standard format. SOAP is one of many protocols used to support service-oriented architectures (SOAs).

Software development process: The procedures and mechanisms by which software applications are specified, designed, developed, tested, and deployed. This process also must define who has authority to make decisions. It is closely related to IT governance.

Source code: The human-readable code that is used to build a program, which a computer can execute. Source code is written in a human-readable programming language such as Java, C, or C++, and translated into "machine code" or "binary code" before being executed by the computer.

Source control system: A system for storing and sharing all of the development assets for a project (source code, tests, etc.). This keeps track of the literally millions of changes that are made day by day to the entire system. It allows you to go back and see exactly what was changed when, and if there is a problem introduced, it allows you to go back to an earlier working version.

Web service: A *unit of work* (as opposed to a complete application) that performs a self-contained activity or action. A Web service makes itself available over a network and uses a standard protocol to talk to other systems over the network.

NOTES

Chapter 1: Success Depends on Innovation and Innovation Depends on Information Technology

Page 8: The top five crucial business goals for 2008 are based on a poll of 353 C-level executives on the *BusinessWeek* Market Advisory Board. The poll was part of *BusinessWeek* Research Services' ongoing series of C-level executive surveys.

Page 14: Fred Brooks's classic *The Mythical Man-Month: Essays on Software Engineering* was originally published in 1975. Addison-Wesley Professional issued an anniversary edition in 1995. This anniversary edition includes the "No Silver Bullet" article, which was originally published in *Proceedings of the IFIP Tenth World Computing Conference*, pp. 1069–1076, 1986.

Pages 17 and 18: Scott Rosenberg, *Dreaming in Code* (New York: Crown Publishers, 2007).

Page 25: The description of the Los Angeles Unified School District's payroll system debacle is from Joel Rubin's "Payroll System Beset from Day 1" article, which appeared in the *Los Angeles Times* on February 11, 2008 (www.latimes.com/news/local/la-me-payroll11feb11,1,1699379.story).

Page 25: The comment from Marla Eby was quoted by Michael Krigsman in an October 2007 post on *ZDNet* (http://blogs.zdnet.com/projectfailures/?p=431). Krigsman is CEO of Asuret, Inc., a software and consulting company dedicated to reducing software implementation failures.

Chapter 2: Who Is Driving Your IT Strategy?

Pages 45 and 46: The comments from Michael Blake were culled from an extensive interview with him conducted in July 2007.

Pages 46 and 47: Ron Rose's quotes were extracted from interviews conducted by phone and via email in 2007 and 2008.

Page 48: The anecdote about Kaiser was gleaned from a 2006 article in *Baseline* magazine by Doug Bartholomew (http://www.baselinemag.com/c/a/Projects-Integration/Requirements-Management-Kaiser-Permanentes-Rx-for-Better-Projects/).

Page 48: The quote attributed to Karl E. Wiegers is from Chapter 2 of his excellent book, *More About Software Requirements: Thorny Issues and Practical Advice* (Redmond, WA: Microsoft Press, 2006).

Page 51: The quotes from Commissioner Paul Cosgrave of the New York City Department of Information Technology and Telecommunications were excerpted from an extensive telephone interview conducted with him in July 2007.

Pages 51 and 52: The quotes from Paul Johnson, president of Kelley Blue Book, were culled from a July 2007 telephone interview with him.

Chapter 3: Read My Lips: IT Is an Asset

Page 60: Mark Lutchen, *Managing IT as a Business* (Hoboken, NJ: John Wiley & Sons, 2003).

Chapter 4: Achieving a Quantum Leap in Developer Productivity

Page 80: For a more in-depth, technical discussion of the Automated Defect Prevention (ADP) methodology, see Dorota Huizinga and Adam Kolawa's *Automated Defect Prevention: Best Practices in Software Management* (Hoboken, NJ: John Wiley & Sons, 2007).

Page 103: For a look at the Feature Creep in action, see the *Dilbert* series from February 5, 2001 to February 7, 2001 (www.dilbert.com/strips).

Chapter 5: The SOA Imperative

Page 113: Rick Levine, Christopher Locke, Doc Searls, and David Weinberger, *The Cluetrain Manifesto: The End of Business as Usual* (New York: Basic Books, 2000).

Chapter 6: Achieving a Quantum Leap in Enterprise Productivity

Page 144: Philip J. Windley's article, "Governing SOA: Rules of the Game," was published in *InfoWorld's IT Strategy Guide* (http://akamai.infoworld.com/pdf/whitepaper/06SGsoagov.pdf).

ABOUT THE AUTHOR

Adam Kolawa holds a Ph.D. in theoretical physics from the California Institute of Technology, and has been granted 16 patents for his recent inventions. In 2001, he was awarded the Los Angeles Ernst & Young's Entrepreneur of the Year Award in the software category. In 2007, *eWeek* recognized him as one of the 100 Most Influential People in IT.

Kolawa is the coauthor of *Bulletproofing Web Applications* (Hungry Minds, 2001) and *Automated Defect Prevention: Best Practices in Software Management* (Wiley, 2007). He has contributed to and written over 100 commentary pieces and technical articles for publications such as the *Wall Street Journal, CIO, Computerworld, Dr. Dobb's Journal,* and *IEEE Computer.* He is the author of numerous scientific papers on physics and parallel processing. Kolawa's work has been featured on CNN, CNBC, BBC, and NPR.

Kolawa is CEO and cofounder of Parasoft, a respected global provider of software solutions and services that help organizations deliver better business applications faster by establishing quality as a continuous process throughout the software development life cycle. Based in Monrovia, California, Parasoft has offices in New York, London, Tokyo, and Shanghai.

INDEX

"n" refers to notes; "f" to figure; **bold** to definition.

177